# Chapter 1: Introduction to Graphics Programming

## Section 1.1: Understanding Graphics APIs

Graphics programming is a fascinating field that deals with creating and manipulating visual elements on a computer screen. To work effectively in this domain, it's essential to understand Graphics Application Programming Interfaces (APIs) and their role in enabling developers to harness the power of graphics hardware.

At its core, a Graphics API is a set of functions and tools that allows developers to interact with the graphics hardware of a computer. These APIs serve as intermediaries between the application and the graphics hardware, providing a way to specify what needs to be drawn, how it should be rendered, and where it should appear on the screen.

Graphics APIs come in various flavors, each with its own strengths and purposes. Some of the most commonly used graphics APIs include OpenGL, Vulkan, DirectX, Metal, and WebGL, among others. These APIs are designed to work on different platforms and cater to various requirements, making them suitable for a wide range of applications, from video games to scientific simulations and more.

One of the primary purposes of a Graphics API is to abstract the complexities of the underlying hardware. Graphics hardware varies significantly across different devices and platforms, so developers can't directly manipulate the hardware registers. Instead, they rely on the Graphics API to handle these details and provide a unified interface. ### Benefits of Using Graphics APIs

Using a Graphics API offers several advantages: 1. **Cross-Platform Compatibility:** Graphics APIs are often designed to work across multiple platforms, allowing developers to write code that can run on various operating systems without major modifications. 2. **Hardware Abstraction:** Graphics APIs abstract the underlying hardware, making it easier to write code that works on different GPUs and graphics cards. 3. **Performance Optimization:** These APIs are optimized for efficient rendering, taking advantage of hardware acceleration to achieve high frame rates and smooth visuals. 4. **Community and Resources:** Popular Graphics APIs like OpenGL and Vulkan have large and active developer communities, which means access to extensive documentation, tutorials, and support. 5. **Rich Feature Sets:** Graphics APIs provide a wealth of features for rendering, including support for 2D and 3D graphics, texturing, shading, and more. ### History of Graphics APIs

Graphics APIs have evolved significantly over the years, adapting to the changing landscape of hardware and software development. Understanding their historical context can provide insights into their design principles and usage.

Early graphics APIs were relatively simplistic and closely tied to specific hardware. For example, the first versions of OpenGL were developed by Silicon Graphics Inc. (SGI) in the 1980s and were tightly integrated with SGI's graphics workstations. These APIs were not designed for general-purpose use.

As the demand for graphics accelerated, there was a need for standardized APIs that could work across different hardware platforms. This led to the development of OpenGL, which aimed to provide a cross-platform, vendor-neutral solution. OpenGL has since become one of the most widely adopted graphics APIs, with versions tailored for various platforms, including desktop, mobile, and web.

In recent years, Vulkan has emerged as a low-level, high-performance graphics API designed to provide more direct control over the hardware. Vulkan is known for its efficiency and flexibility, making it a popular choice for demanding applications and games.

With this historical context in mind, it's clear that graphics APIs have come a long way from their early beginnings. Today, developers have a range of options to choose from, each offering unique features and capabilities. ### Conclusion

In this section, we've introduced the concept of Graphics APIs and discussed their significance in graphics programming. We've also touched on the benefits of using these APIs, their history, and how they've evolved to meet the demands of modern graphics development.

As we delve deeper into this book, we'll explore specific graphics APIs like OpenGL and Vulkan in more detail, providing you with the knowledge and tools you need to become proficient in graphics programming. Whether you're a game developer, a scientist working on simulations, or simply curious about the world of graphics, understanding these APIs is a crucial step toward achieving your goals.

## Section 1.2: Evolution of OpenGL and Vulkan

The world of graphics programming has seen significant evolution over the years, with two prominent players, OpenGL and Vulkan, standing out as pivotal technologies. In this section, we'll delve into the evolution of these graphics APIs, highlighting their historical development and key milestones. ### The Birth of OpenGL

OpenGL, short for "Open Graphics Library," was born in the early 1990s as a project by Silicon Graphics Inc. (SGI). Its initial purpose was to provide a standardized, cross-platform graphics API for SGI's own high-performance workstations. OpenGL 1.0 was released in 1992, and it marked the beginning of OpenGL's journey as a widely adopted graphics API.

OpenGL's success can be attributed to its open standard nature, which allowed other hardware and software vendors to implement their own OpenGL drivers. This openness led to the rapid adoption of OpenGL across various platforms, making it a go-to choice for 3D graphics programming. Over the years, OpenGL evolved, with multiple versions and extensions adding new features and capabilities. ### The Need for a Low-Level Alternative: Vulkan Emerges

While OpenGL was successful, it had limitations, particularly in terms of performance and efficiency. As hardware became more complex, there was a growing demand for a low-level graphics API that provided more direct control over the underlying hardware.

Vulkan, developed by the Khronos Group, emerged as the answer to this demand. It was officially released in 2016 and represented a significant departure from the high-level abstraction of OpenGL. Vulkan was designed with modern hardware in mind, offering explicit control over memory management, parallelism, and more.

One of the key motivations behind Vulkan's development was to reduce driver overhead. In OpenGL, drivers often performed many behind-the-scenes tasks, which could lead to inefficiencies. Vulkan, on the other hand, shifted more of this responsibility to the application developer, allowing for better performance optimization. ### Key Differences and Advantages

Vulkan and OpenGL have distinct differences: - **Explicit Control:** Vulkan offers explicit control over many aspects of graphics programming, giving developers more responsibility but also more power to optimize for performance. - **Multi-threading:** Vulkan was designed with multi-threading in mind, allowing developers to take full advantage of modern CPUs with multiple cores. - **Cross-Platform:** Like OpenGL, Vulkan is designed to be cross-platform and can run on various operating systems, including Windows, Linux, and Android. - **Performance:** Vulkan's low-level design and efficient use of resources make it a preferred choice for high-performance applications, including games. ### Choosing Between OpenGL and Vulkan

Choosing between OpenGL and Vulkan depends on the specific needs of your project. If you're working on a project with straightforward graphics requirements or targeting older hardware, OpenGL may be a more accessible option due to its higher-level abstractions. However, if you're developing a performance-critical application for modern hardware, Vulkan's explicit control and efficiency may be more appealing.

Ultimately, the choice between OpenGL and Vulkan should consider the project's goals, the target hardware, and the development team's familiarity with each API. ### Conclusion

In this section, we've explored the evolution of OpenGL and the emergence of Vulkan as low-level, high-performance graphics APIs. Both APIs have played crucial roles in the world of graphics programming, each with its own strengths and purposes. Understanding their historical development and key differences is essential for choosing the right tool for your graphics programming endeavors.

## Section 1.3: Setting Up Your Development Environment

Setting up a proper development environment is a crucial step in graphics programming, as it directly impacts your ability to write, test, and debug code. In this section, we will walk through the essential components and considerations for setting up a graphics programming environment. ### Choice of Operating System

The first decision to make when setting up your development environment is choosing an operating system. Graphics programming is platform-agnostic to some extent, with APIs like OpenGL and Vulkan designed to work across different operating systems. However, your choice of OS can still influence your development experience. - **Windows:** Windows is a popular choice for graphics development due to its wide user base and support for a variety of graphics hardware. It offers a range of development tools and IDEs, making it accessible for many developers. - **Linux:** Linux is a preferred platform for many graphics programmers, especially those working on open-source projects. It provides excellent control over system resources and is a common choice for server-side graphics applications. - **macOS:** macOS is commonly used by developers working on applications for Apple devices. It supports OpenGL and Metal, Apple's graphics API. ### Development Tools and IDEs

Choosing the right development tools and Integrated Development Environments (IDEs) can greatly enhance your productivity. Here are some options: - **Visual Studio:** Visual Studio is a widely used IDE for Windows development. It offers excellent support for C/C++ and integrates well with graphics APIs like OpenGL. - **Visual Studio Code:** Visual Studio Code (VS Code) is a lightweight, cross-platform code editor that is popular among developers. It supports a wide range of programming languages and offers extensions for graphics programming. - **CLion:** CLion is a powerful IDE developed by JetBrains that is known for its C/C++ support. It is available for Windows, Linux, and macOS. ### Graphics API SDKs

To work with graphics APIs like OpenGL or Vulkan, you'll need the corresponding SDKs. These SDKs provide header files, libraries, and tools necessary for graphics development. - **OpenGL SDK:** Setting up OpenGL typically involves installing the OpenGL SDK for your platform. It includes header files and libraries, and you may need to configure your development environment to link to them correctly. - **Vulkan SDK:** Vulkan has its SDK, which provides the necessary tools and libraries for Vulkan development. It's available for multiple platforms and comes with useful validation layers for debugging. ### Graphics Drivers

Up-to-date graphics drivers are essential for ensuring your code works correctly with your hardware. Graphics drivers are responsible for translating API calls into instructions that the graphics hardware can execute. Make sure to keep your graphics drivers updated to access the latest features and bug fixes. ### Version Control and Project Organization

Using version control systems like Git is essential for managing your graphics programming projects. Git allows you to track changes, collaborate with others, and easily revert to previous versions if issues arise. Organize your projects into a clear directory structure to keep your codebase clean and maintainable. ### Setting Up a Build System

A robust build system is crucial for compiling and linking your graphics code. Popular build systems like CMake and Makefile are commonly used in graphics programming. They help automate the compilation process and manage dependencies. ### Hardware Considerations

Graphics programming often demands a system with sufficient graphics processing power. Ensure that your hardware meets the requirements for the graphics API and applications you intend to develop. High-performance GPUs are essential for real-time rendering and complex simulations. ### Conclusion

In this section, we've discussed the essential components and considerations for setting up your graphics programming development environment. Choosing the right operating system, development tools, SDKs, graphics drivers, version control, project organization, build system, and hardware are key factors that can significantly impact your productivity and the success of your graphics projects. A well-configured development environment is the foundation for creating stunning visuals and efficient graphics applications.

## Section 1.4: Basics of 2D and 3D Rendering

Understanding the fundamentals of 2D and 3D rendering is at the core of graphics programming. In this section, we'll explore the basic concepts and techniques behind rendering graphics in both two and three dimensions. ### 2D Rendering

2D rendering involves creating images or scenes that exist within a flat, two-dimensional space. It's the foundation for many graphics applications, including user interfaces, 2D games, and vector graphics. Here are some key concepts and techniques: - **Coordinate Systems:** In 2D rendering, a common coordinate system is used, where (0,0) typically represents the top-left corner of the screen or viewport. Positive x values extend to the right, and positive y values extend downward. - **Primitives:**

Primitives are basic shapes used in 2D rendering, such as points, lines, and polygons. Drawing these primitives forms the basis of 2D graphics. - **Color and Textures:** Colors and textures are applied to 2D shapes to give them visual properties. Colors are specified using RGB values, and textures are 2D images that can be mapped onto shapes. - **Blending:** Blending is a technique that allows the combination of colors from multiple objects or layers, producing effects like transparency and shadows. - **Transformations:** Transformations, such as translation, rotation, scaling, and shearing, are applied to 2D objects to position them within the coordinate space or create animations. - **Rasterization:** Rasterization is the process of converting vector-based graphics (lines, curves, etc.) into pixel-based representations for display on a screen. - **Anti-Aliasing:** Anti-aliasing techniques are used to smooth jagged edges and reduce visual artifacts in rendered 2D images. ### 3D Rendering

3D rendering involves creating images or scenes that exist within a three-dimensional space. It's essential for 3D games, simulations, architectural visualization, and more. Here are some key concepts and techniques: - **3D Coordinate Systems:** In 3D rendering, a 3D Cartesian coordinate system is used, with x, y, and z axes. Objects exist in a 3D space, and their positions are specified using three coordinates. - **Meshes and Models:** 3D objects are represented as meshes composed of vertices, edges, and faces. These meshes are often used to construct complex 3D models. - **Cameras:** Cameras are used to define the viewpoint and perspective of the scene. They determine what portion of the 3D world is visible in the rendered image. - **Lighting:** Lighting plays a crucial role in 3D rendering, affecting how objects appear in a scene. Techniques like ambient, diffuse, and specular lighting are used to simulate the interaction of light with surfaces. - **Shaders:** Shaders are small programs that run on the GPU and control various aspects of rendering, including vertex processing, fragment shading, and more. They are essential for achieving realistic 3D graphics. - **Texture Mapping:** Texture mapping involves applying 2D images (textures) to the surfaces of 3D objects to add details and realism. - **Depth and Z-**

**Buffering:** Depth and z-buffering techniques are used to determine which parts of a 3D scene are visible and should be rendered. - **Rendering Pipelines:** Modern 3D graphics pipelines consist of various stages, including vertex processing, tessellation, geometry shading, rasterization, and fragment shading. Understanding these stages is crucial for efficient 3D rendering. ### Conclusion

In this section, we've explored the basics of 2D and 3D rendering in graphics programming. These fundamental concepts are essential for creating visuals in a wide range of applications, from simple 2D user interfaces to complex 3D game worlds. As you delve deeper into graphics programming, you'll build upon these principles and learn more advanced techniques to create stunning and interactive graphics.

## Section 1.5: Common Graphics Terminology

In the world of graphics programming, there is a rich set of terminology that you'll encounter frequently. Understanding these terms is essential for effective communication and for grasping the intricacies of graphics development. Let's explore some common graphics terminology: ### Pixels

A pixel, short for "picture element," is the smallest unit of a digital image. Each pixel represents a single point in an image and is characterized by its color or grayscale value. Pixels are arranged in a grid to create the visual content on a screen or in an image file. The resolution of a display or image is often described in terms of the number of pixels it contains, such as "1920x1080" for Full HD resolution. ### Rasterization

Rasterization is the process of converting vector-based graphics or 3D models into a grid of pixels for display. It involves determining which pixels should be filled or shaded to represent the objects in the scene. Rasterization is a fundamental step in rendering 2D and 3D graphics. ### Rendering

Rendering refers to the process of generating a final image or frame from a 3D scene. It encompasses various tasks, including lighting calculations, shading, texturing, and rasterization. The result of rendering is the visual output that is displayed on a screen or saved as an image or video. ### Shader

A shader is a small program that runs on the graphics processing unit (GPU) and is responsible for determining the appearance of a pixel or vertex in a 3D scene. Shaders can control aspects like color, lighting, and texture mapping. Vertex shaders process vertex data, while fragment shaders handle pixel-level operations. ### Texture

A texture is a 2D image that is applied to the surfaces of 3D models or used in 2D graphics. Textures can add details, patterns, and realism to objects in a scene. They are commonly used for materials like wood, metal, or fabric, as well as for applying images to 3D models. ### Framebuffer

A framebuffer, often referred to as a render target, is a region of memory that stores the final rendered image or frame. It contains color information, depth information, and other data necessary for rendering. The contents of the framebuffer are displayed on the screen or used as a source for further rendering operations. ### Anti-Aliasing

Anti-aliasing is a technique used to reduce the appearance of jagged edges in digital images. It works by smoothing out the transitions between pixels, resulting in a smoother and more visually pleasing image. Common anti-aliasing methods include supersampling and multisampling. ### Vertex

In 3D graphics, a vertex is a point in space defined by its 3D coordinates (x, y, z). Vertices are the building blocks of 3D models and are connected by edges to form polygons. Each vertex can store additional attributes like color, texture coordinates, and normals. ### Normals

Normals are vectors that are perpendicular to the surface of a 3D object at a specific point (vertex). They play a crucial role in lighting calculations, determining how light interacts with the surface. Normals are used to calculate the direction and intensity of reflected light. ### Ray Tracing

Ray tracing is a rendering technique that simulates the behavior of light rays as they interact with objects in a 3D scene. It is known for producing highly realistic images with accurate lighting and reflections. Ray tracing is computationally intensive but has become more practical with advancements in hardware and software. ### Conclusion

In this section, we've explored common graphics terminology that forms the foundation of graphics programming. Familiarizing yourself with these terms is essential for effective communication and for diving deeper into the world of graphics development. As you continue your journey in graphics programming, you'll encounter these concepts regularly, and a solid understanding of them will be invaluable.

# Chapter 2: Getting Started with OpenGL

## Section 2.1: OpenGL Fundamentals

OpenGL, short for "Open Graphics Library," is a widely used graphics API for rendering 2D and 3D graphics. In this section, we'll delve into the fundamentals of OpenGL, understanding its architecture, key concepts, and how to set up a basic OpenGL application. ### Overview of OpenGL

OpenGL is not a single library but a specification that defines a set of functions and behaviors for rendering graphics. It provides a cross-platform and vendor-neutral interface for interacting with graphics hardware. Applications communicate with OpenGL through API calls to perform various rendering tasks.

OpenGL operates as a state machine, where the current state settings affect the outcome of rendering operations. Developers can set various parameters, such as the color, texture, and transformation, before issuing rendering commands. ### The OpenGL Rendering Pipeline

Understanding the rendering pipeline is essential for working effectively with OpenGL. The pipeline consists of several stages that transform 3D data into a 2D image. Here's a simplified overview: 1. **Vertex Specification:** The process begins by specifying the 3D vertices of objects. Each vertex includes its position and attributes. 2. **Vertex Shader:** Vertex shader programs are executed for each vertex, allowing for transformations, lighting calculations, and attribute interpolation. 3. **Primitive Assembly:** OpenGL assembles vertices into primitives such as points, lines, or triangles. 4. **Geometry Shader (Optional):** The geometry shader, if used, can generate additional vertices or modify existing ones. 5. **Rasterization:** Primitives are rasterized, meaning they are converted into fragments (potential pixels). 6. **Fragment Shader:** Fragment shader programs determine the final color and other attributes of each fragment. 7. **Per-Fragment Operations:** These operations include depth testing, blending, and stencil testing. 8. **Framebuffer:** The final image is rendered to the framebuffer, which can then be displayed on the screen or used for further processing. ### OpenGL State and Objects

OpenGL manages rendering through various objects and state variables. Some essential objects and concepts include: - **OpenGL Context:** An OpenGL context represents a rendering state. Each application can have one or more contexts, but only one can be active at a time. - **OpenGL Buffers:** Buffers are used to store vertex data, texture data, and other types of data. Common types of buffers include vertex buffer objects (VBOs) and framebuffer objects (FBOs). - **OpenGL Shaders:** Shaders are programs written in OpenGL Shading Language (GLSL) that run on the GPU. Vertex and fragment shaders are the most commonly used types. - **OpenGL Textures:** Textures are 2D or 3D images used for applying surface detail to 3D objects. They can be used for color, normal maps, and more. - **OpenGL Framebuffers:** Framebuffers are used for off-screen rendering and can be used to render to textures or multiple render targets. ### Setting Up an OpenGL Application

To get started with OpenGL programming, you'll need to set up a development environment and create a basic OpenGL application. Here are the general steps: 1. **Initialize OpenGL Context:** Create an OpenGL context using platform-specific libraries or frameworks. 2. **Load and Compile Shaders:** Write and compile vertex and fragment shaders using GLSL. 3. **Create Buffers and Objects:** Set up vertex buffers, texture buffers, and other OpenGL objects. 4. **Set OpenGL State:** Configure the OpenGL state, including viewport size, clear color, and depth testing settings. 5. **Main Loop:** Create a main rendering loop that repeatedly renders frames, handling user input and updates. 6. **Render Objects:** In the main loop, bind shaders, set uniforms, and render objects using OpenGL commands. 7. **Swap Buffers:** Swap the front and back buffers to display the rendered image. ### Conclusion

In this section, we've introduced the fundamentals of OpenGL, including its architecture, rendering pipeline, state management, and setting up a basic OpenGL application. As you continue to explore OpenGL, you'll dive deeper into each aspect, learning how to create intricate graphics and interactive applications. Understanding these basics is crucial for building a strong foundation in OpenGL programming.

## Section 2.2: Creating Your First OpenGL Application

Creating your first OpenGL application is an exciting step in your journey as a graphics programmer. In this section, we'll walk through the essential steps and code snippets needed to set up a basic OpenGL application that renders a simple triangle on the screen. ### Prerequisites

Before you begin, make sure you have an OpenGL development environment set up. You should have access to an OpenGL context and a suitable development environment or IDE. You'll also need the necessary libraries and headers for OpenGL.### Initializing OpenGL

The first step is to initialize an OpenGL context. The exact process may vary depending on your platform, but the general idea is to create a window or rendering surface and create a context associated with it. Here's an example using the popular GLFW library for window creation:

```
#include <GLFW/glfw3.h>

int main() {
    // Initialize GLFW
    if (!glfwInit()) {
        return -1;
    }

    // Create a windowed mode window and its OpenGL context
    GLFWwindow* window = glfwCreateWindow(800, 600, "OpenGL Window", NULL, NULL);
    if (!window) {
        glfwTerminate();
        return -1;
    }

    // Make the window's context current
    glfwMakeContextCurrent(window);

    // Main rendering loop goes here

    // Terminate GLFW when finished
    glfwTerminate();
    return 0;
}
```

### Setting Up GLEW

To use modern OpenGL features, you often need a library like GLEW (OpenGL Extension Wrangler Library) to manage extensions. You can initialize GLEW after creating the OpenGL context:

```c
#include <GL/glew.h>

int main() {
    // ... Previous code ...

    // Initialize GLEW
    GLenum err = glewInit();
    if (err != GLEW_OK) {
        fprintf(stderr, "GLEW Error: %s\n",
glewGetErrorString(err));
        return -1;
    }

    // Check for OpenGL version and extensions
    if (!GLEW_VERSION_3_3) {
        fprintf(stderr, "OpenGL 3.3 is not
supported.\n");
        return -1;
    }

    // ... Main rendering loop and other OpenGL code
...

    glfwTerminate();
    return 0;
}
```

## Creating a Simple Triangle

Now, let's render a simple triangle on the screen. We'll define the vertices, compile shaders, and use them to draw the triangle.

```c
// Vertex shader source code
const char* vertexShaderSource = R"(
    #version 330 core
    layout (location = 0) in vec3 aPos;
    void main() {
        gl_Position = vec4(aPos.x, aPos.y, aPos.z,
1.0);
    }
)";
```

```cpp
// Fragment shader source code
const char* fragmentShaderSource = R"(
    #version 330 core
    out vec4 FragColor;
    void main() {
        FragColor = vec4(1.0f, 0.5f, 0.2f, 1.0f);
    }
)";

int main() {
    // ... Previous code ...

    // Vertex data for a simple triangle
    float vertices[] = {
        -0.5f, -0.5f, 0.0f,  // Bottom-left corner
         0.5f, -0.5f, 0.0f,  // Bottom-right corner
         0.0f,  0.5f, 0.0f   // Top-center corner
    };

    // Create and compile the vertex shader
    GLuint vertexShader =
glCreateShader(GL_VERTEX_SHADER);
    glShaderSource(vertexShader, 1,
&vertexShaderSource, NULL);
    glCompileShader(vertexShader);

    // Create and compile the fragment shader
    GLuint fragmentShader =
glCreateShader(GL_FRAGMENT_SHADER);
    glShaderSource(fragmentShader, 1,
&fragmentShaderSource, NULL);
    glCompileShader(fragmentShader);

    // Create a shader program and link the shaders
    GLuint shaderProgram = glCreateProgram();
    glAttachShader(shaderProgram, vertexShader);
    glAttachShader(shaderProgram, fragmentShader);
    glLinkProgram(shaderProgram);
    glUseProgram(shaderProgram);
```

```cpp
    // Create and bind a Vertex Array Object (VAO)
    GLuint VAO, VBO;
    glGenVertexArrays(1, &VAO);
    glGenBuffers(1, &VBO);

    glBindVertexArray(VAO);
    glBindBuffer(GL_ARRAY_BUFFER, VBO);
    glBufferData(GL_ARRAY_BUFFER, sizeof(vertices),
vertices, GL_STATIC_DRAW);

    // Configure vertex attribute pointers
    glVertexAttribPointer(0, 3, GL_FLOAT, GL_FALSE, 3 *
sizeof(float), (void*)0);
    glEnableVertexAttribArray(0);

    // Render loop
    while (!glfwWindowShouldClose(window)) {
        // Clear the screen
        glClear(GL_COLOR_BUFFER_BIT);

        // Draw the triangle
        glBindVertexArray(VAO);
        glDrawArrays(GL_TRIANGLES, 0, 3);

        // Swap front and back buffers
        glfwSwapBuffers(window);

        // Poll for and process events
        glfwPollEvents();
    }

    // ... Cleanup code ...

    return 0;
}
```

In this code snippet, we define the vertex and fragment shaders, create and compile them, and then create a shader program. We also set up vertex data for a simple triangle, create a Vertex Array Object (VAO), and configure the vertex attribute pointers.

Finally, we enter a rendering loop where we clear the screen, draw the triangle, and swap buffers.

This basic example provides a glimpse into the process of setting up an OpenGL application and rendering a simple object. As you progress in OpenGL programming, you'll explore more advanced rendering techniques and create more complex scenes.

## Section 2.3: Rendering Primitives

Rendering primitives is a fundamental aspect of OpenGL programming. Primitives are the basic building blocks for creating 2D and 3D graphics. In this section, we'll explore various types of primitives and how to render them in OpenGL. ### Types of Primitives

OpenGL supports several types of primitives, each serving a different purpose in graphics programming: 1. **Points:** Points are the simplest primitives and represent individual pixels. They are often used for particle systems or as markers in various applications. 2. **Lines:** Lines are composed of two points and can be used to create shapes, wireframes, and other geometric elements. 3. **Line Strips:** Line strips are a series of connected line segments. They are useful for creating continuous lines or paths. 4. **Triangles:** Triangles are the most common primitive used in 3D graphics. They are composed of three vertices and are used to construct 3D models and surfaces. 5. **Triangle Strips:** Triangle strips are a series of connected triangles, where each new triangle shares an edge with the previous one. They are more efficient for rendering large surfaces. 6. **Triangle Fans:** Similar to triangle strips, triangle fans connect triangles in a circular pattern around a central vertex. They are often used for rendering objects with radial symmetry. ### Rendering Primitives in OpenGL

To render primitives in OpenGL, you typically follow these steps: 1. **Define Vertex Data:** Create an array of vertices that define the positions of the primitive's points. Each vertex should include at least position data. 2. **Create Buffers:** Generate

OpenGL buffers (e.g., Vertex Buffer Objects or VBOs) to store the vertex data. 3. **Bind Buffers:** Bind the VBOs to the OpenGL context, making the data available for rendering. 4. **Specify Vertex Attributes:** Define how the vertex data is structured, including attribute sizes and offsets. 5. **Set Up Shaders:** Compile and link vertex and fragment shaders to control the appearance of the primitive. 6. **Render:** Use OpenGL rendering commands to draw the primitive, specifying the type (e.g., GL_POINTS, GL_LINES, GL_TRIANGLES) and the number of vertices to use.

Here's a simplified example of rendering a triangle:

```
// Vertex data for a triangle
float vertices[] = {
    -0.5f, -0.5f, 0.0f,  // Vertex 1
     0.5f, -0.5f, 0.0f,  // Vertex 2
     0.0f,  0.5f, 0.0f   // Vertex 3
};

// Create and bind VBO
unsigned int VBO;
glGenBuffers(1, &VBO);
glBindBuffer(GL_ARRAY_BUFFER, VBO);

// Copy vertex data to the VBO
glBufferData(GL_ARRAY_BUFFER, sizeof(vertices),
vertices, GL_STATIC_DRAW);

// Create and compile shaders (not shown here)

// Set up vertex attributes (position attribute)
glVertexAttribPointer(0, 3, GL_FLOAT, GL_FALSE, 3 *
sizeof(float), (void*)0);
glEnableVertexAttribArray(0);

// Use the shader program
glUseProgram(shaderProgram);

// Render the triangle
glDrawArrays(GL_TRIANGLES, 0, 3);
```

This code sets up a VBO, copies vertex data to it, specifies vertex attributes, and renders a triangle using a shader program. Similar steps can be applied to other types of primitives. ### Conclusion

Rendering primitives is a fundamental concept in OpenGL programming. Whether you're creating simple points, lines, or complex 3D models composed of triangles, understanding how to define, buffer, and render these primitives is essential. As you advance in graphics programming, you'll explore more advanced techniques for creating stunning visuals and interactive experiences.

## Section 2.4: Transformations and Matrices

Transformations play a crucial role in graphics programming as they allow you to position, scale, rotate, and manipulate objects in a 2D or 3D scene. Matrices are commonly used to represent these transformations. In this section, we'll explore how transformations and matrices work in OpenGL. ### Understanding Transformations

Transformations in OpenGL involve changing the position, orientation, and scale of objects in a scene. There are three primary types of transformations: 1. **Translation:** Translation moves an object from one location to another in a specified direction and distance. In 2D graphics, this is often used for animation and object placement. 2. **Rotation:** Rotation changes the orientation of an object around a specified axis. It is used to achieve effects like spinning objects, camera rotations, and realistic animations. 3. **Scaling:** Scaling changes the size of an object along one or more axes. Scaling can be uniform (scaling in all directions equally) or non-uniform (scaling in different directions). ### Transformation Matrices

In OpenGL, transformations are typically represented using 4x4 matrices. These matrices can combine multiple transformations into a single matrix, allowing for complex transformations.

The most common transformation matrices are: 1. **Model Matrix (Model-View Matrix):** This matrix defines the transformation from an object's local coordinate space to the world coordinate space. It includes translations, rotations, and scalings applied to individual objects. 2. **View Matrix:** The view matrix represents the transformation applied to the camera or the viewer's perspective. It controls the position and orientation of the camera in the scene. 3. **Projection Matrix:** The projection matrix defines how the 3D scene is projected onto a 2D screen. It controls perspective and can be set to represent orthographic or perspective projections. 4. **Model-View-Projection (MVP) Matrix:** This is the combination of the model, view, and projection matrices. It is used to transform object coordinates into screen coordinates. ### Applying Transformations

To apply transformations in OpenGL, you typically follow these steps: 1. **Create Transformation Matrices:** Create model, view, and projection matrices based on the desired transformations. You can use libraries like GLM (OpenGL Mathematics) to simplify matrix operations. 2. **Pass Matrices to Shader:** Send the transformation matrices to your shader program as uniform variables. This allows the shader to apply the transformations to each vertex. 3. **In the Vertex Shader:** In the vertex shader, transform the vertex positions using the transformation matrices. This can be done by multiplying the vertex position with the model, view, and projection matrices to obtain the final position in clip coordinates. 4. **Combine Matrices:** In the shader, you can combine the model, view, and projection matrices to create the MVP matrix and apply it to the vertex positions.

Here's a simplified example of how to set up and use transformation matrices in OpenGL:

```
// Create transformation matrices using GLM (not shown
here)

// Pass matrices to the shader
glUseProgram(shaderProgram);
glUniformMatrix4fv(modelLoc, 1, GL_FALSE,
```

```
glm::value_ptr(modelMatrix));
glUniformMatrix4fv(viewLoc, 1, GL_FALSE,
glm::value_ptr(viewMatrix));
glUniformMatrix4fv(projectionLoc, 1, GL_FALSE,
glm::value_ptr(projectionMatrix));

// In the vertex shader
#version 330 core
layout (location = 0) in vec3 aPos;

uniform mat4 model;
uniform mat4 view;
uniform mat4 projection;

void main() {
    mat4 mvp = projection * view * model;
    gl_Position = mvp * vec4(aPos, 1.0);
}
```

This code demonstrates the process of creating transformation matrices, passing them to the shader, and applying them to vertex positions. ### Conclusion

Transformations and matrices are fundamental concepts in OpenGL programming, enabling you to create dynamic and visually appealing graphics. Whether you're animating objects, controlling camera views, or setting up perspective projections, a solid understanding of transformations and matrices is essential for manipulating and positioning objects in your scenes. As you delve further into graphics programming, you'll explore advanced techniques and use these concepts to create complex and interactive 2D and 3D graphics.

## Section 2.5: Shaders and Vertex Buffers

Shaders and vertex buffers are essential components of OpenGL that play a central role in rendering graphics. In this section, we'll explore shaders, their types, and how they interact with vertex buffers to create dynamic and visually appealing graphics. ### Shaders in OpenGL

Shaders are small programs that run on the GPU and are responsible for various aspects of rendering, such as vertex transformations, lighting calculations, and pixel color determination. OpenGL uses shaders to define how objects in a scene should be rendered.

The main types of shaders in OpenGL are: 1. **Vertex Shaders:** Vertex shaders operate on each vertex in a 3D model and are responsible for transforming the vertices from object space to camera space. They can perform operations like translation, rotation, and scaling. 2. **Fragment Shaders:** Fragment shaders, also known as pixel shaders, determine the final color of each pixel on a rendered object. They handle lighting, texture mapping, and shading calculations. 3. **Geometry Shaders (Optional):** Geometry shaders operate on entire primitives (e.g., triangles) and can create new vertices, discard primitives, or modify existing ones. They are optional and not always used in OpenGL applications. ### Writing Shaders

Shaders in OpenGL are typically written in a language called GLSL (OpenGL Shading Language). GLSL is C-like and provides specific syntax and functions for vertex and fragment shaders.

Here's a simplified example of a vertex shader that transforms vertices:

```glsl
#version 330 core
layout (location = 0) in vec3 aPos;  // Input vertex position

uniform mat4 model;       // Model matrix
uniform mat4 view;        // View matrix
uniform mat4 projection;  // Projection matrix

void main() {
    mat4 mvp = projection * view * model;
    gl_Position = mvp * vec4(aPos, 1.0);  // Final transformed vertex position
}
```

And here's an example of a fragment shader that determines pixel color:

```
#version 330 core
out vec4 FragColor;  // Output color

void main() {
    FragColor = vec4(1.0f, 0.5f, 0.2f, 1.0f);  // Set
pixel color to orange
}
```

**Compiling and Linking Shaders**

To use shaders in an OpenGL program, you must compile and link them into a shader program. Here's a simplified example of how to compile and link shaders using the OpenGL API:

```
// Create and compile vertex shader
GLuint vertexShader = glCreateShader(GL_VERTEX_SHADER);
glShaderSource(vertexShader, 1, &vertexShaderSource,
NULL);
glCompileShader(vertexShader);

// Create and compile fragment shader
GLuint fragmentShader =
glCreateShader(GL_FRAGMENT_SHADER);
glShaderSource(fragmentShader, 1,
&fragmentShaderSource, NULL);
glCompileShader(fragmentShader);

// Create shader program and link shaders
GLuint shaderProgram = glCreateProgram();
glAttachShader(shaderProgram, vertexShader);
glAttachShader(shaderProgram, fragmentShader);
glLinkProgram(shaderProgram);
glUseProgram(shaderProgram);
```

Once shaders are compiled and linked into a shader program, you can use that program to render objects. ### Vertex Buffers and Vertex Arrays

Vertex buffers and vertex arrays are used to store and organize vertex data that define the geometry of 3D models. Vertex buffers (VBOs) store the actual vertex data, while vertex arrays (VAOs) store the configuration of the data, including attribute pointers.

Here's a simplified example of creating and using VBOs and VAOs:

```
// Create and bind VAO
GLuint VAO;
glGenVertexArrays(1, &VAO);
glBindVertexArray(VAO);

// Create and bind VBO
GLuint VBO;
glGenBuffers(1, &VBO);
glBindBuffer(GL_ARRAY_BUFFER, VBO);

// Copy vertex data to VBO
glBufferData(GL_ARRAY_BUFFER, sizeof(vertices),
vertices, GL_STATIC_DRAW);

// Specify vertex attribute pointers
glVertexAttribPointer(0, 3, GL_FLOAT, GL_FALSE, 3 *
sizeof(float), (void*)0);
glEnableVertexAttribArray(0);

// Bind the VAO for use
glBindVertexArray(VAO);

// ... Render code using VAO ...

// Clean up (unbind VAO and VBO)
glBindVertexArray(0);
```

In this code, we create a VAO, bind it, create a VBO, and bind it as well. We then copy vertex data to the VBO, specify vertex attribute pointers, and enable the attributes. Finally, we bind the VAO before rendering. ### Conclusion

Shaders and vertex buffers are fundamental to OpenGL programming, allowing you to define how objects are rendered and store the geometry of 3D models efficiently. By writing and compiling shaders, you gain control over vertex and pixel-level operations, while VBOs and VAOs help organize and manage vertex data. Understanding how shaders and vertex buffers work together is essential for creating sophisticated graphics in OpenGL. As you delve further into graphics programming, you'll explore more advanced shader techniques and data organization strategies to achieve your desired visual effects.

# Chapter 3: Advanced OpenGL Techniques

## Section 3.1: Lighting and Shading

Lighting and shading are fundamental aspects of rendering in computer graphics. They are responsible for determining how objects in a scene appear, including how they interact with light sources and their surroundings. In this section, we'll delve into the concepts of lighting and shading in OpenGL. ### Understanding Lighting

Lighting in computer graphics simulates the interaction between light sources and surfaces. It allows you to create realistic or stylized illumination effects in your 3D scenes. OpenGL supports several lighting models, with two primary types: 1. **Ambient Lighting:** Ambient lighting represents the constant, uniform illumination present in a scene. It doesn't depend on the direction of light sources or the orientation of surfaces. Ambient lighting provides a basic level of brightness to all objects, even in shadowed areas. 2. **Diffuse and Specular Lighting:** Diffuse and specular lighting are directional and depend on the orientation of surfaces relative to light sources. Diffuse lighting represents the scattering of light in all directions on a rough surface, while specular lighting models the reflection of light off smooth surfaces, creating highlights. ### Phong Lighting Model

The Phong lighting model is a widely used lighting model in computer graphics, and it consists of three components: 1. **Ambient Term:** The ambient term provides the base color of an object in the absence of direct light. It is typically represented as a constant color value. 2. **Diffuse Term:** The diffuse term simulates the scattering of light on a surface, and its intensity varies based on the angle between the light source and the surface normal. It results in soft shading. 3. **Specular Term:** The specular term represents the highlights on a surface when light is reflected in a specific direction. It depends on the viewer's position, light direction, and the surface's smoothness. ### Shading in OpenGL

Shading in OpenGL is achieved through vertex and fragment shaders. Here's a simplified example of how to implement the Phong lighting model in shaders:

```glsl
#version 330 core
in vec3 FragPos;    // Fragment position in world
coordinates
in vec3 Normal;     // Normal vector at the fragment
in vec3 LightPos;   // Position of the light source

uniform vec3 lightColor;
uniform vec3 objectColor;
uniform vec3 viewPos;

out vec4 FragColor;

void main() {
    // Ambient lighting
    float ambientStrength = 0.1;
    vec3 ambient = ambientStrength * lightColor;

    // Diffuse lighting
    vec3 norm = normalize(Normal);
    vec3 lightDir = normalize(LightPos - FragPos);
    float diff = max(dot(norm, lightDir), 0.0);
    vec3 diffuse = diff * lightColor;
```

```glsl
// Specular lighting
float specularStrength = 0.5;
vec3 viewDir = normalize(viewPos - FragPos);
vec3 reflectDir = reflect(-lightDir, norm);
float spec = pow(max(dot(viewDir, reflectDir),
0.0), 32.0);
vec3 specular = specularStrength * spec *
lightColor;

vec3 result = (ambient + diffuse + specular) *
objectColor;
FragColor = vec4(result, 1.0);
}
```

This fragment shader calculates ambient, diffuse, and specular lighting components and combines them to determine the final pixel color. ### Implementation in OpenGL

To implement lighting and shading in OpenGL, you need to set up shaders, define lighting properties, and render objects accordingly. This often involves specifying the position and color of light sources, setting material properties, and managing shaders.

In addition to implementing basic lighting models like Phong, you can explore more advanced techniques such as normal mapping, shadow mapping, and environment mapping to achieve sophisticated lighting effects. ### Conclusion

Lighting and shading are essential components of creating realistic and visually appealing 3D graphics in OpenGL. By understanding the principles of lighting models like Phong and implementing them using shaders, you gain the ability to control how light interacts with surfaces in your scenes. As you advance in graphics programming, you'll explore advanced lighting techniques and optimization strategies to create stunning visual experiences in your OpenGL applications.

## Section 3.2: Texturing and Texture Mapping

Texturing is a fundamental technique in computer graphics that allows you to apply images, patterns, or surface details to 3D objects, making them appear more realistic and visually appealing. Texture mapping is the process of applying textures to objects in a scene. In this section, we'll explore texturing and texture mapping in OpenGL. ### Understanding Textures

A texture is a 2D image that can be applied to the surface of 3D objects in OpenGL. Textures can contain various information, such as colors, patterns, bump maps, and more. They are often used to simulate real-world materials and add detail to objects.

Textures can be classified into different types based on their purpose: 1. **Diffuse Textures:** These textures define the base color of an object. They determine how light interacts with the object's surface. 2. **Normal Maps:** Normal maps encode surface normals to simulate fine surface details, such as bumps and dents. They affect how light is reflected off the surface. 3. **Specular Maps:** Specular maps control the intensity of specular highlights on an object's surface. They determine where the surface appears shinier or more reflective. 4. **Height Maps:** Height maps encode height information, often used for terrain generation or displacement mapping. ### Texture Coordinates

To apply a texture to a 3D object, you need texture coordinates that map points on the object's surface to corresponding points on the texture. These coordinates are often expressed as (u, v) or (s, t) coordinates and range from 0.0 to 1.0.

In OpenGL, you can assign texture coordinates to each vertex of a 3D model. During rendering, the texture coordinates are interpolated across the surface of the object, allowing you to map the texture accurately. ### Loading Textures

OpenGL itself does not provide built-in functionality for loading image files, so you'll typically use external libraries like SOIL, DevIL, or stb_image to load texture images. These libraries can handle various image formats, such as JPEG, PNG, and BMP.

Here's a simplified example of how to load and bind a texture in OpenGL using the stb_image library:

```cpp
// Load texture image
int width, height, nrChannels;
unsigned char* data = stbi_load("texture.jpg", &width,
&height, &nrChannels, 0);

// Generate and bind a texture
GLuint textureID;
glGenTextures(1, &textureID);
glBindTexture(GL_TEXTURE_2D, textureID);

// Set texture filtering and wrapping options
glTexParameteri(GL_TEXTURE_2D, GL_TEXTURE_MIN_FILTER,
GL_LINEAR);
glTexParameteri(GL_TEXTURE_2D, GL_TEXTURE_MAG_FILTER,
GL_LINEAR);
glTexParameteri(GL_TEXTURE_2D, GL_TEXTURE_WRAP_S,
GL_REPEAT);
glTexParameteri(GL_TEXTURE_2D, GL_TEXTURE_WRAP_T,
GL_REPEAT);

// Load texture data into OpenGL
glTexImage2D(GL_TEXTURE_2D, 0, GL_RGB, width, height,
0, GL_RGB, GL_UNSIGNED_BYTE, data);
glGenerateMipmap(GL_TEXTURE_2D);

// Free loaded image data
stbi_image_free(data);
```

**Texture Mapping in Shaders**

Once you've loaded a texture, you can use it in your shaders to apply it to objects. In the fragment shader, you can access the texture and interpolate texture coordinates to determine the pixel color for each fragment.

Here's a simplified example of texture mapping in a fragment shader:

```glsl
#version 330 core
in vec2 TexCoord;     // Texture coordinates
out vec4 FragColor;

uniform sampler2D texture1;   // Texture object

void main() {
    // Sample the texture using interpolated texture
coordinates
    FragColor = texture(texture1, TexCoord);
}
```

In this shader, the `sampler2D` uniform represents the texture, and the `texture()` function is used to sample the texture using the interpolated texture coordinates (`TexCoord`) to determine the final fragment color. ### Conclusion

Texturing and texture mapping are fundamental techniques in OpenGL that enhance the visual realism of 3D graphics. By applying textures to objects, you can simulate materials and surface details, making scenes more immersive and engaging. Understanding how to load textures, assign texture coordinates, and use them in shaders is crucial for creating visually appealing graphics in OpenGL. As you advance in graphics programming, you'll explore more complex texture mapping techniques and ways to optimize texture usage for better performance and realism.

## Section 3.3: Framebuffers and Render Targets

Framebuffers and render targets are essential concepts in OpenGL that allow you to perform advanced rendering techniques and post-processing effects. In this section, we'll explore what framebuffers and render targets are and how they can be used to achieve various rendering effects. ### Understanding Framebuffers

A framebuffer is a data structure in OpenGL that represents an off-screen rendering target. It's essentially a container for storing pixel data that can be used for various purposes, including rendering to textures, applying post-processing effects, or creating shadow maps.

In OpenGL, a framebuffer can consist of multiple attachments, such as color attachments, depth attachments, and stencil attachments. These attachments store different types of data during rendering. ### Render Targets

Render targets are specific attachments within a framebuffer that store rendering results. The most common types of render targets are: 1. **Color Attachments:** These store the color information of the rendered scene. You can have multiple color attachments in a single framebuffer to render to multiple textures simultaneously, which is useful for techniques like deferred rendering. 2. **Depth Attachment:** This attachment stores the depth information, which is crucial for depth testing and shadow mapping. It determines which objects are visible and occluded in the scene. 3. **Stencil Attachment:** The stencil attachment is used to store stencil values, which can be used for more advanced rendering techniques, like stencil shadows and masks. ### Using Framebuffers and Render Targets

To use framebuffers and render targets in OpenGL, you need to follow these steps: 1. **Create a Framebuffer Object (FBO):** Create an FBO using `glGenFramebuffers()`. This creates a framebuffer object that you can attach render targets to. 2. **Bind the FBO:** Bind the FBO using `glBindFramebuffer()`. This makes the FBO the current rendering target. 3. **Attach Render Targets:** Attach render targets (textures or renderbuffers) to the FBO using `glFramebufferTexture2D()` or `glFramebufferRenderbuffer()`. You can attach color attachments, depth attachments, and stencil attachments as needed. 4. **Render to the FBO:** Perform rendering operations, and OpenGL will draw into the attached render targets instead of the screen. 5. **Unbind the FBO:** After rendering is complete, unbind the FBO using `glBindFramebuffer(GL_FRAMEBUFFER, 0)` to make the default framebuffer (the screen) the rendering target again.

Here's a simplified example of using a framebuffer to render to a texture:

```cpp
// Create a framebuffer object
GLuint framebuffer;
glGenFramebuffers(1, &framebuffer);
glBindFramebuffer(GL_FRAMEBUFFER, framebuffer);

// Create and attach a texture as a color attachment
GLuint texture;
glGenTextures(1, &texture);
glBindTexture(GL_TEXTURE_2D, texture);
glTexImage2D(GL_TEXTURE_2D, 0, GL_RGB, screenWidth,
screenHeight, 0, GL_RGB, GL_UNSIGNED_BYTE, NULL);
glTexParameteri(GL_TEXTURE_2D, GL_TEXTURE_MIN_FILTER,
GL_LINEAR);
glTexParameteri(GL_TEXTURE_2D, GL_TEXTURE_MAG_FILTER,
GL_LINEAR);
glFramebufferTexture2D(GL_FRAMEBUFFER,
GL_COLOR_ATTACHMENT0, GL_TEXTURE_2D, texture, 0);

// Check framebuffer completeness
if (glCheckFramebufferStatus(GL_FRAMEBUFFER) !=
GL_FRAMEBUFFER_COMPLETE)
    std::cout << "Framebuffer is not complete!" <<
std::endl;

// Render to the framebuffer (set shaders and draw
objects)

// Unbind the framebuffer
glBindFramebuffer(GL_FRAMEBUFFER, 0);
```

After rendering to the framebuffer, the texture attached as a color attachment will contain the rendered image. ### Post-Processing Effects

One of the primary uses of framebuffers and render targets is to apply post-processing effects. After rendering the scene to a framebuffer, you can use a fullscreen quad and shaders to apply effects like blur, bloom, depth of field, and color grading to the final image before displaying it to the screen.

This approach allows you to separate rendering from post-processing and create visually stunning effects without modifying the original scene geometry. ### Conclusion

Framebuffers and render targets are powerful tools in OpenGL that enable you to perform advanced rendering techniques and achieve visually appealing effects. By rendering to off-screen targets, you can implement post-processing effects and separate the rendering pipeline from the final image displayed on the screen. Understanding how to create and use framebuffers and render targets is essential for advanced graphics programming in OpenGL.

## Section 3.4: Vertex Array Objects (VAOs) and Vertex Buffer Objects (VBOs)

Vertex Array Objects (VAOs) and Vertex Buffer Objects (VBOs) are essential components in OpenGL that help organize and manage vertex data efficiently. In this section, we'll explore what VAOs and VBOs are and how they are used in OpenGL graphics programming. ### Vertex Buffer Objects (VBOs)

A Vertex Buffer Object (VBO) is a buffer that holds vertex data, such as positions, colors, normals, and texture coordinates. Instead of storing vertex data in system memory (RAM), VBOs store this data in the GPU's memory, which is faster to access during rendering.

To create and use a VBO in OpenGL, you typically follow these steps: 1. **Generate a VBO:** Use glGenBuffers() to generate a VBO object. 2. **Bind the VBO:** Bind the VBO using glBindBuffer() to specify that subsequent operations should affect this VBO. 3. **Allocate and Upload Data:** Allocate memory for the vertex data using glBufferData(), and upload the vertex data to the VBO. 4. **Specify Vertex Attributes:** Define the format of the vertex data using glVertexAttribPointer(). This tells OpenGL how to interpret the data in the VBO. 5. **Enable Vertex**

**Attributes:** Enable the vertex attributes using `glEnableVertexAttribArray()` to make them accessible in vertex shaders. 6. **Draw Objects:** Use the VBO to draw objects efficiently with `glDrawArrays()` or `glDrawElements()`.

Here's a simplified example of creating and using a VBO:

```
// Generate and bind a VBO
GLuint VBO;
glGenBuffers(1, &VBO);
glBindBuffer(GL_ARRAY_BUFFER, VBO);

// Allocate and upload vertex data
glBufferData(GL_ARRAY_BUFFER, sizeof(vertices),
vertices, GL_STATIC_DRAW);

// Specify vertex attribute pointers
glVertexAttribPointer(0, 3, GL_FLOAT, GL_FALSE, 6 *
sizeof(float), (void*)0);
glEnableVertexAttribArray(0);

glVertexAttribPointer(1, 3, GL_FLOAT, GL_FALSE, 6 *
sizeof(float), (void*)(3 * sizeof(float)));
glEnableVertexAttribArray(1);

// ... Bind VBO and draw objects ...
```

### Vertex Array Objects (VAOs)

A Vertex Array Object (VAO) is an OpenGL object that stores the configuration of vertex attributes. It helps streamline the process of switching between different sets of vertex data and vertex formats. VAOs act as containers for VBOs and attribute pointers, making it easier to manage multiple objects with varying vertex data.

To use a VAO, you typically follow these steps: 1. **Generate a VAO:** Use `glGenVertexArrays()` to generate a VAO object. 2. **Bind the VAO:** Bind the VAO using `glBindVertexArray()` to specify that subsequent attribute and VBO operations should affect this VAO. 3. **Bind and Configure VBOs:** Bind the VBO(s) containing vertex data and specify their attribute pointers. This associates the VBOs with the VAO. 4. **Enable Vertex Attributes:** Enable the vertex attributes using `glEnableVertexAttribArray()` within the VAO to make them accessible in vertex shaders. 5. **Draw Objects:** Bind the VAO and use it to draw objects efficiently with `glDrawArrays()` or `glDrawElements()`.

Here's a simplified example of creating and using a VAO:

```
// Generate and bind a VAO
GLuint VAO;
glGenVertexArrays(1, &VAO);
glBindVertexArray(VAO);

// Bind and configure VBO(s) and attribute pointers
glBindBuffer(GL_ARRAY_BUFFER, VBO);
glVertexAttribPointer(0, 3, GL_FLOAT, GL_FALSE, 6 *
sizeof(float), (void*)0);
glEnableVertexAttribArray(0);

glVertexAttribPointer(1, 3, GL_FLOAT, GL_FALSE, 6 *
sizeof(float), (void*)(3 * sizeof(float)));
glEnableVertexAttribArray(1);

// ... Bind VAO and draw objects ...
```

Using VAOs simplifies the process of managing multiple VBOs and their associated vertex attribute configurations, making your OpenGL code more organized and efficient. ### Benefits of VAOs and VBOs

VAOs and VBOs offer several advantages in OpenGL programming: - **Improved Performance:** Storing vertex data in GPU memory and efficiently managing it using VBOs can significantly boost rendering performance. - **Code Organization:** VAOs help organize vertex attribute configurations, making it easier to switch between different sets of vertex data. - **Reduced OpenGL Calls:** By storing attribute pointers and vertex data configurations in VAOs, you can reduce

the number of OpenGL calls needed to render objects. ###
Conclusion

Vertex Array Objects (VAOs) and Vertex Buffer Objects (VBOs)
are crucial components in OpenGL for managing and rendering
vertex data efficiently. VBOs store vertex data in GPU memory,
while VAOs help organize and configure the data's layout.
Understanding how to create, bind, and use VAOs and VBOs is
essential for optimizing and organizing your OpenGL graphics
programming code. These objects streamline the process of
rendering complex scenes with multiple objects and varying
vertex data formats.

## Section 3.5: Implementing 3D Models

In computer graphics, rendering 3D models is a fundamental
task, and OpenGL provides the tools and techniques necessary to
display 3D objects in a 3D scene. In this section, we'll explore
how to implement 3D models in OpenGL, covering concepts like
model loading, transformation matrices, and rendering. ###
Loading 3D Models

To render 3D models in OpenGL, you need to load their
geometry and material properties. 3D models are often stored in
various file formats, such as OBJ, FBX, or glTF. You can use
libraries like Assimp or custom parsers to read these files and
extract the model's information, including vertex positions,
normals, texture coordinates, and materials.

Here's a simplified example of loading a 3D model using the
Assimp library:

```cpp
// Load a 3D model using Assimp
Assimp::Importer importer;
const aiScene* scene = importer.ReadFile("model.obj",
aiProcess_Triangulate | aiProcess_FlipUVs);

if (!scene || scene->mFlags & AI_SCENE_FLAGS_INCOMPLETE
|| !scene->mRootNode) {
    std::cerr << "Error: " << importer.GetErrorString()
```

```
    << std::endl;
        return;
}
```

```
// Process the model data (vertices, normals, textures,
etc.) from 'scene'
```

Transformation Matrices

Transformations are crucial for positioning, rotating, and scaling 3D models in a scene. OpenGL uses transformation matrices to perform these operations. The common transformation matrices are: 1. **Model Matrix:** The model matrix represents the transformation of a model from its local space to world space. It includes translation, rotation, and scaling. 2. **View Matrix:** The view matrix defines the camera's position and orientation in the world space. It transforms the world to the camera's view. 3. **Projection Matrix:** The projection matrix controls the camera's perspective or orthographic projection. It transforms the view to the screen space.

By combining these matrices in the vertex shader, you can achieve the desired positioning and projection of 3D models in your scene. ### Rendering 3D Models

To render 3D models, you'll typically iterate through the model's components, such as meshes, and render them one by one. For each mesh, you'll bind the appropriate textures, set shader uniforms for material properties, apply transformation matrices, and issue draw calls.

Here's a simplified example of rendering a 3D model's mesh:

```
// Set shader uniforms (model, view, projection
matrices, material properties)
shader.use();
shader.setMat4("model", modelMatrix);
shader.setMat4("view", viewMatrix);
shader.setMat4("projection", projectionMatrix);
shader.setVec3("material.ambient", ambientColor);
shader.setVec3("material.diffuse", diffuseColor);
```

```
shader.setVec3("material.specular", specularColor);
shader.setFloat("material.shininess", shininess);

// Bind textures (diffuse, specular, normal, etc.)
glBindTexture(GL_TEXTURE_2D, texture1);
glBindTexture(GL_TEXTURE_2D, texture2);

// Render the mesh
mesh.render();
```

This code sets up the necessary shader uniforms, binds textures, and renders a mesh using the specified transformation matrices and material properties. ### Optimization Considerations

When rendering multiple 3D models or complex scenes, optimization becomes essential. Techniques like frustum culling, level of detail (LOD), and instancing can significantly improve rendering performance. Additionally, using a scene graph to organize and manage objects in your scene can simplify rendering and enable more complex interactions. ### Conclusion

Implementing 3D models in OpenGL involves loading model data, using transformation matrices to position and project models, and rendering them with appropriate shaders and materials. Understanding these concepts is fundamental for creating 3D graphics in OpenGL and is the basis for building complex 3D scenes and applications. As you advance in graphics programming, you can explore more advanced rendering techniques and optimizations to achieve impressive visual results.

# Chapter 4: Understanding Vulkan

## Section 4.1: Introduction to Vulkan

Vulkan is a modern, low-level graphics and compute API developed by the Khronos Group. It provides developers with explicit control over the GPU and is designed for high performance, efficiency, and parallelism. In this section, we'll introduce Vulkan and explore its key features and advantages. ### Key Features of Vulkan #### 1. Explicit Control:

One of Vulkan's defining features is its explicit control over GPU resources. Unlike high-level graphics APIs like OpenGL, which manage many aspects of rendering automatically, Vulkan requires developers to specify almost every detail of the rendering process. This level of control allows for fine-grained optimization and is especially beneficial for applications where performance is critical. #### 2. Cross-Platform:

Vulkan is designed to work across multiple platforms, including Windows, Linux, Android, and more. This cross-platform support makes it an attractive choice for developers aiming to target a wide range of devices and operating systems. #### 3. Multi-threading and Parallelism:

Vulkan is designed to take full advantage of multi-core CPUs. It allows developers to create multiple threads to perform rendering tasks in parallel. This parallelism can significantly improve performance on modern processors with multiple cores. #### 4. Lower Overhead:

Vulkan minimizes CPU overhead by reducing the driver's role in managing graphics resources. This results in lower API-related CPU usage, which is particularly valuable for CPU-bound applications. #### 5. Modern Graphics Features:

Vulkan supports modern graphics features, including tessellation, geometry shaders, and compute shaders. This allows developers to create visually stunning and highly complex graphics effects. #### 6. Fine-grained Memory Management:

Developers have precise control over memory allocation and management in Vulkan. This fine-grained memory control enables efficient memory usage and reduces memory-related bottlenecks. ### Vulkan Layers

Vulkan introduces the concept of layers, which are optional components that can be inserted into the Vulkan API stack. Layers can provide validation, debugging, and additional functionality. Validation layers, in particular, are crucial during development as they help identify and diagnose errors in Vulkan applications. ### Vulkan Extensions

Vulkan extensions provide additional functionality beyond the core Vulkan API. They are platform-specific and allow developers to access features that may not be present in all Vulkan implementations. Vulkan extensions enable compatibility with various GPU vendors and hardware features. ### Vulkan vs. OpenGL

Compared to OpenGL, Vulkan offers several advantages, including better performance, lower CPU overhead, and more control. However, Vulkan also requires more code to accomplish tasks that OpenGL handles automatically. Choosing between Vulkan and OpenGL depends on the specific requirements and goals of your graphics application. ### Setting Up Vulkan Development Environment

To start using Vulkan, you'll need a development environment that includes the Vulkan SDK, which provides the necessary headers, libraries, and tools. Vulkan SDKs are available for various platforms, and you can install them according to your development needs.

In the next sections, we'll delve deeper into Vulkan's low-level approach, setting up a Vulkan application, and understanding Vulkan instances and devices. With this foundation, you'll be well-equipped to explore the capabilities of Vulkan and harness its power for graphics programming.

## Section 4.2: Vulkan's Low-Level Approach

Vulkan's low-level approach is one of its defining characteristics and a key reason for its performance and efficiency. In this section, we'll delve into the low-level aspects of Vulkan and understand how it differs from higher-level graphics APIs like OpenGL. ### Explicit Control over GPU

Vulkan gives developers explicit control over GPU resources, which means you have to specify nearly every detail of the rendering process. While this might seem daunting at first, it offers significant advantages. With explicit control, you can fine-tune your application to make the most efficient use of GPU resources.

In contrast, higher-level APIs like OpenGL abstract many details and manage resources automatically. While this abstraction simplifies development, it can also lead to inefficiencies, especially in scenarios where you need precise control over rendering. ### Abstraction Layers

In OpenGL, there are abstraction layers that handle tasks like shader compilation, pipeline management, and resource allocation. These layers hide many complexities from developers, making it easier to create graphics applications quickly. However, this abstraction comes at a cost – higher CPU overhead and potentially reduced performance.

In Vulkan, you're responsible for managing these aspects yourself. For example, you'll compile shaders, define pipelines, and allocate memory explicitly. This hands-on approach allows you to eliminate unnecessary overhead and optimize your application for specific use cases. ### Validation Layers

Vulkan's validation layers are a valuable tool during development. They help you identify and fix errors in your Vulkan code, ensuring that your application behaves correctly. These layers catch issues like incorrect API usage, memory leaks, and synchronization problems.

Validation layers are optional, but they're highly recommended during development. Once you're confident in your code's correctness, you can disable them for production builds to reduce runtime overhead. ### Multi-threading and Parallelism

Vulkan is designed for multi-threading and parallelism from the ground up. You can create multiple threads to perform rendering tasks concurrently. This is particularly useful on modern processors with multiple CPU cores, as it allows you to distribute rendering workloads efficiently.

In contrast, OpenGL's design was originally single-threaded, although some extensions and approaches enable multi-threading. Vulkan's native support for parallelism makes it well-suited for applications that require high performance and utilize modern CPU architectures effectively. ### Reduced Driver Overhead

OpenGL drivers are responsible for managing many aspects of rendering, including resource allocation and state tracking. This can lead to unpredictable CPU overhead, as driver implementations vary between GPU vendors.

Vulkan reduces driver overhead by shifting more responsibility to the application. You have greater control over resource management, which can lead to more predictable performance and lower CPU usage. ### Summary

Vulkan's low-level approach provides developers with explicit control over GPU resources, reduces CPU overhead, and allows for efficient multi-threading and parallelism. While it requires more code and effort compared to higher-level APIs like OpenGL, Vulkan's performance benefits and flexibility make it an excellent choice for graphics programming, especially in applications where every ounce of performance matters. Understanding Vulkan's low-level design is essential for harnessing its power and building high-performance graphics applications.

## Section 4.3: Setting Up Vulkan Development Environment

Setting up a Vulkan development environment is the first step to start working with this powerful graphics and compute API. In this section, we'll guide you through the process of preparing

your development environment for Vulkan programming. ###
Vulkan SDK Installation

The Vulkan Software Development Kit (SDK) is a crucial
component for Vulkan development. It includes the Vulkan
headers, libraries, and tools necessary for building Vulkan
applications. Here are the general steps to install the Vulkan
SDK: 1. **Visit the Khronos Group Website:** Go to the official
Khronos Group website (https://www.khronos.org/vulkan/ )
and navigate to the Vulkan SDK download section. 2. **Download
the SDK:** Download the Vulkan SDK appropriate for your
platform (Windows, Linux, macOS, etc.). Be sure to download the
latest version to ensure you have access to the most up-to-date
features and bug fixes. 3. **Installation:** Follow the installation
instructions provided with the SDK. The installation process may
vary depending on your platform. ### Development
Environment

To start writing Vulkan applications, you need a development
environment with a compatible compiler and build system. Here
are some considerations based on popular development
platforms: #### Windows: - **Compiler:** Microsoft Visual C++
(MSVC) or MinGW-w64 with GCC. - **IDE:** Visual Studio with
Vulkan SDK integration is a common choice for Windows
development. - **Build System:** CMake is often used for cross-
platform Vulkan projects. #### Linux: - **Compiler:** GCC or Clang.
- **IDE:** You can use various code editors like Visual Studio Code
or IDEs like CLion. Command-line development is also common
on Linux. - **Build System:** CMake is widely used on Linux for
Vulkan projects. #### macOS: - **Compiler:** Clang. - **IDE:** Xcode
with Vulkan SDK integration can be used. - **Build System:** CMake
or Xcode project files. ### Vulkan Headers and Libraries

Once you have the Vulkan SDK installed, you can access the
Vulkan headers and libraries necessary for development. These
files are typically located in the SDK installation directory. You'll
need to include the Vulkan headers in your code and link against
the Vulkan libraries during compilation. ### Development Tools

While not strictly required, some development tools can help streamline Vulkan development: - **API Documentation:** The Vulkan specification, available on the Khronos Group website, is an essential reference. It provides detailed information about Vulkan's functions, data structures, and usage. - **Validation Layers:** As mentioned in the previous section, validation layers are valuable during development for error checking. You can enable them in your Vulkan application to catch potential issues. - **Vulkan Debuggers:** Tools like RenderDoc and NVIDIA Nsight can be helpful for debugging Vulkan applications. They allow you to inspect Vulkan API calls, resources, and shaders during runtime. ### Vulkan Samples and Tutorials

Learning Vulkan can be challenging, especially if you're new to low-level graphics programming. To get started, you can explore Vulkan samples and tutorials available online. These resources provide hands-on examples and explanations to help you grasp the concepts and best practices of Vulkan programming.

By setting up your Vulkan development environment and familiarizing yourself with the necessary tools and resources, you'll be ready to dive into Vulkan programming and unleash its potential for high-performance graphics and compute applications.

## Section 4.4: Creating a Vulkan Application

Creating a Vulkan application involves several essential steps, from initializing the Vulkan instance to rendering graphics on the screen. In this section, we'll walk through the process of creating a Vulkan application, highlighting key steps along the way. ### 1. Initializing Vulkan

The first step is to initialize the Vulkan instance. The instance is an essential object that serves as the entry point for all Vulkan operations. To create an instance, you must specify application information, such as the application name and version, and request any required Vulkan extensions.

```cpp
VkApplicationInfo appInfo = {};
appInfo.sType = VK_STRUCTURE_TYPE_APPLICATION_INFO;
appInfo.pApplicationName = "My Vulkan App";
appInfo.applicationVersion = VK_MAKE_VERSION(1, 0, 0);
appInfo.pEngineName = "No Engine";
appInfo.engineVersion = VK_MAKE_VERSION(1, 0, 0);
appInfo.apiVersion = VK_API_VERSION_1_0;

VkInstanceCreateInfo createInfo = {};
createInfo.sType =
VK_STRUCTURE_TYPE_INSTANCE_CREATE_INFO;
createInfo.pApplicationInfo = &appInfo;

// Specify required extensions (e.g., for surface and
platform-specific functionality)
createInfo.enabledExtensionCount =
requiredExtensions.size();
createInfo.ppEnabledExtensionNames =
requiredExtensions.data();

VkInstance instance;
if (vkCreateInstance(&createInfo, nullptr, &instance)
!= VK_SUCCESS) {
    throw std::runtime_error("Failed to create Vulkan
instance!");
}
```

Selecting a Physical Device

After creating the instance, you need to select a physical device
(GPU) to work with. Vulkan supports multiple GPUs on a single
system, so you must choose the one that best suits your needs.
You can enumerate available devices and select the most
suitable one based on your criteria, such as GPU capabilities,
memory, and features.

```cpp
uint32_t deviceCount = 0;
vkEnumeratePhysicalDevices(instance, &deviceCount,
nullptr);
if (deviceCount == 0) {
    throw std::runtime_error("No Vulkan-compatible GPUs
```

```
found!");
}

std::vector<VkPhysicalDevice> devices(deviceCount);
vkEnumeratePhysicalDevices(instance, &deviceCount,
devices.data());

VkPhysicalDevice physicalDevice = VK_NULL_HANDLE;
for (const auto& device : devices) {
    if (isDeviceSuitable(device)) {
        physicalDevice = device;
        break;
    }
}
```

## Creating a Logical Device

Once you've selected a physical device, you can create a logical
device. The logical device represents an interface to interact with
the chosen GPU. You can specify the device features and
extensions you want to use.

```
VkDeviceQueueCreateInfo queueCreateInfo = {};
queueCreateInfo.sType =
VK_STRUCTURE_TYPE_DEVICE_QUEUE_CREATE_INFO;
queueCreateInfo.queueFamilyIndex = queueFamilyIndex;
queueCreateInfo.queueCount = 1;
float queuePriority = 1.0f;
queueCreateInfo.pQueuePriorities = &queuePriority;

VkDeviceCreateInfo createInfo = {};
createInfo.sType =
VK_STRUCTURE_TYPE_DEVICE_CREATE_INFO;
createInfo.pQueueCreateInfos = &queueCreateInfo;
createInfo.queueCreateInfoCount = 1;
createInfo.pEnabledFeatures = &deviceFeatures;
createInfo.enabledExtensionCount =
deviceExtensions.size();
createInfo.ppEnabledExtensionNames =
deviceExtensions.data();
```

```
VkDevice device;
if (vkCreateDevice(physicalDevice, &createInfo,
nullptr, &device) != VK_SUCCESS) {
    throw std::runtime_error("Failed to create Vulkan
logical device!");
}
```

## Creating a Vulkan Surface

To render graphics to a window or surface, you need to create a
Vulkan surface. The way you create a surface depends on the
platform and windowing system you're using. For example, on
Windows, you can use the Win32 API, while on Linux, you might
use the X Window System (Xlib) or other platform-specific
methods.

```
VkSurfaceKHR surface;
if (glfwCreateWindowSurface(instance, window, nullptr,
&surface) != VK_SUCCESS) {
    throw std::runtime_error("Failed to create Vulkan
window surface!");
}
```

## Creating Swap Chain

A swap chain is a series of images that Vulkan uses to display the
final rendered image to the screen. Creating a swap chain
involves specifying its properties, such as image format and
presentation mode, to match the capabilities of the surface and
the desired rendering quality.

```
SwapChainSupportDetails swapChainSupport =
querySwapChainSupport(physicalDevice);
VkSurfaceFormatKHR surfaceFormat =
chooseSwapSurfaceFormat(swapChainSupport.formats);
VkPresentModeKHR presentMode =
chooseSwapPresentMode(swapChainSupport.presentModes);
VkExtent2D extent =
chooseSwapExtent(swapChainSupport.capabilities);

VkSwapchainCreateInfoKHR createInfo = {};
createInfo.sType =
```

```cpp
VK_STRUCTURE_TYPE_SWAPCHAIN_CREATE_INFO_KHR;
createInfo.surface = surface;
createInfo.minImageCount = imageCount;
createInfo.imageFormat = surfaceFormat.format;
createInfo.imageColorSpace = surfaceFormat.colorSpace;
createInfo.imageExtent = extent;
createInfo.imageArrayLayers = 1;
createInfo.imageUsage =
VK_IMAGE_USAGE_COLOR_ATTACHMENT_BIT;

if (graphicsFamily != presentFamily) {
    createInfo.imageSharingMode =
VK_SHARING_MODE_CONCURRENT;
    createInfo.queueFamilyIndexCount = 2;
    uint32_t queueFamilyIndices[] = { graphicsFamily,
presentFamily };
    createInfo.pQueueFamilyIndices =
queueFamilyIndices;
} else {
    createInfo.imageSharingMode =
VK_SHARING_MODE_EXCLUSIVE;
}

createInfo.preTransform =
swapChainSupport.capabilities.currentTransform;
createInfo.compositeAlpha =
VK_COMPOSITE_ALPHA_OPAQUE_BIT_KHR;
createInfo.presentMode = presentMode;
createInfo.clipped = VK_TRUE;
createInfo.oldSwapchain = VK_NULL_HANDLE;

VkSwapchainKHR swapChain;
if (vkCreateSwapchainKHR(device, &createInfo, nullptr,
&swapChain) != VK_SUCCESS) {
    throw std::runtime_error("Failed to create Vulkan
swap chain!");
}
```

## Creating Swap Chain Images and Image Views

Once the swap chain is created, you can retrieve the images it uses and create image views for them. Image views allow you to access the images and use them as render targets.

```
vkGetSwapchainImagesKHR(device, swapChain, &imageCount,
nullptr);
std::vector<VkImage> swapChainImages(imageCount);
vkGetSwapchainImagesKHR(device, swapChain, &imageCount,
swapChainImages.data());

std::vector<VkImageView>
swapChainImageViews(swapChainImages.size());
for (size_t i = 0; i < swapChainImages.size(); i++) {
    swapChainImageViews[i] =
createImageView(swapChainImages[i],
surfaceFormat.format);
}
```

## Creating a Render Pass

A render pass describes the structure of a frame in your application. It specifies the number and types of attachments (e.g., color and depth) and the rendering operations (e.g., clear, load, and store) for each attachment. Creating a render pass is a crucial step in Vulkan rendering.

```
VkAttachmentDescription colorAttachment = {};
colorAttachment.format = surfaceFormat.format;
colorAttachment.samples = VK_SAMPLE_COUNT_1_BIT;
colorAttachment.loadOp = VK_ATTACHMENT_LOAD_OP_CLEAR;
colorAttachment.storeOp = VK_ATTACHMENT_STORE_OP_STORE;
colorAttachment.st
```

# Section 4.5: Vulkan Instance and Devices

In Vulkan, the concept of instances and devices is fundamental to the graphics programming workflow. Instances represent the high-level environment for your Vulkan application, while devices are the interfaces to interact with GPUs. In this section,

we'll delve into the details of Vulkan instances and devices. ###
Vulkan Instances

A Vulkan instance serves as the entry point to the Vulkan API
and represents the global state of your application. You create an
instance to initialize Vulkan and specify parameters like
application information, extensions, and validation layers. Here's
a step-by-step breakdown of creating a Vulkan instance:

```cpp
// Specify application information
VkApplicationInfo appInfo = {};
appInfo.sType = VK_STRUCTURE_TYPE_APPLICATION_INFO;
appInfo.pApplicationName = "My Vulkan App";
appInfo.applicationVersion = VK_MAKE_VERSION(1, 0, 0);
appInfo.pEngineName = "No Engine";
appInfo.engineVersion = VK_MAKE_VERSION(1, 0, 0);
appInfo.apiVersion = VK_API_VERSION_1_0;

// Specify instance creation information
VkInstanceCreateInfo createInfo = {};
createInfo.sType =
VK_STRUCTURE_TYPE_INSTANCE_CREATE_INFO;
createInfo.pApplicationInfo = &appInfo;

// Specify required extensions (e.g., for surface and
platform-specific functionality)
createInfo.enabledExtensionCount =
requiredExtensions.size();
createInfo.ppEnabledExtensionNames =
requiredExtensions.data();

// Specify validation layers (optional but highly
recommended during development)
createInfo.enabledLayerCount = validationLayers.size();
createInfo.ppEnabledLayerNames =
validationLayers.data();

// Create the Vulkan instance
VkInstance instance;
if (vkCreateInstance(&createInfo, nullptr, &instance)
!= VK_SUCCESS) {
```

```
    throw std::runtime_error("Failed to create Vulkan
instance!");
}
```

Vulkan instances allow you to set various parameters, such as the application name, version, and the desired Vulkan extensions and validation layers. Validation layers are particularly helpful during development as they can catch potential issues in your Vulkan code. ### Vulkan Devices

After creating a Vulkan instance, the next step is to select and interact with a physical device (GPU). Vulkan supports multiple GPUs on a single system, and you must choose one to work with. To select a physical device, follow these steps:

```
uint32_t deviceCount = 0;
vkEnumeratePhysicalDevices(instance, &deviceCount,
nullptr);
if (deviceCount == 0) {
    throw std::runtime_error("No Vulkan-compatible GPUs
found!");
}

std::vector<VkPhysicalDevice> devices(deviceCount);
vkEnumeratePhysicalDevices(instance, &deviceCount,
devices.data());

VkPhysicalDevice physicalDevice = VK_NULL_HANDLE;
for (const auto& device : devices) {
    if (isDeviceSuitable(device)) {
        physicalDevice = device;
        break;
    }
}
```

In this code snippet, we first enumerate the available physical devices, and then we choose the most suitable one based on specific criteria. The isDeviceSuitable function evaluates whether a device meets your application's requirements, such as necessary features and capabilities.

Once you've selected a physical device, you can create a logical device associated with it. The logical device serves as the interface for issuing Vulkan commands and managing GPU resources. You can specify the device features and extensions you want to use when creating the logical device.

In summary, Vulkan instances and devices are crucial components of Vulkan graphics programming. Instances represent the global state of your application, while devices provide the means to interact with GPUs. By setting up instances and selecting the appropriate devices, you lay the foundation for building Vulkan applications with explicit control and high performance.

# Chapter 5: Vulkan Commands and Pipelines

## Section 5.1: Vulkan Command Buffers

Vulkan command buffers are essential for issuing rendering and compute commands to the GPU. They play a central role in defining the operations performed during a rendering pass. In this section, we'll explore Vulkan command buffers and their use in graphics programming. ### Overview of Command Buffers

In Vulkan, command buffers are used to record sequences of commands that are later submitted for execution on the GPU. There are primarily two types of command buffers: 1. **Primary Command Buffers:** These are the top-level command buffers and are used to begin a new rendering pass. They can contain secondary command buffers or direct rendering commands. 2. **Secondary Command Buffers:** These command buffers are used to record secondary rendering commands that can be executed within a primary command buffer. They are often employed for rendering objects with complex hierarchies or for implementing reusable rendering techniques. ### Recording Command Buffers

To record commands into a command buffer, you need to start a recording session. This is done by calling `vkBeginCommandBuffer`. You specify the command buffer, a set of flags, and a structure that provides information about the intended usage.

```
VkCommandBufferBeginInfo beginInfo = {};
beginInfo.sType =
VK_STRUCTURE_TYPE_COMMAND_BUFFER_BEGIN_INFO;
beginInfo.flags =
VK_COMMAND_BUFFER_USAGE_SIMULTANEOUS_USE_BIT; //
Specify usage flags

if (vkBeginCommandBuffer(commandBuffer, &beginInfo) !=
VK_SUCCESS) {
    throw std::runtime_error("Failed to begin recording
command buffer!");
}
```

Once the command buffer recording has started, you can record various types of commands, including: - **Drawing commands:** These commands are used to render geometry. For example, `vkCmdDraw` and `vkCmdDrawIndexed` are used to draw vertices. - **Resource binding commands:** You can bind descriptor sets (containing uniforms and textures) using `vkCmdBindDescriptorSets`. - **Pipeline state commands:** Set the active graphics pipeline with `vkCmdBindPipeline`. - **Clearing commands:** Clearing the color, depth, and stencil attachments of the frame buffer can be done with commands like `vkCmdClearColorImage` and `vkCmdClearDepthStencilImage`.
### Ending and Submitting Command Buffers

After recording the necessary commands, you must end the command buffer recording with `vkEndCommandBuffer`. Once a command buffer is in the "ended" state, you can't record any more commands into it.

```
if (vkEndCommandBuffer(commandBuffer) != VK_SUCCESS) {
    throw std::runtime_error("Failed to end recording
```

```
command buffer!");
}
```

To execute the recorded commands on the GPU, you need to submit the command buffer to a queue. This is done using the vkQueueSubmit function.

```
VkSubmitInfo submitInfo = {};
submitInfo.sType = VK_STRUCTURE_TYPE_SUBMIT_INFO;
submitInfo.commandBufferCount = 1;
submitInfo.pCommandBuffers = &commandBuffer;

if (vkQueueSubmit(graphicsQueue, 1, &submitInfo,
VK_NULL_HANDLE) != VK_SUCCESS) {
    throw std::runtime_error("Failed to submit command
buffer to the queue!");
}
```

### Resetting and Reusing Command Buffers

After a command buffer has been submitted and executed, you can reset it for reuse with vkResetCommandBuffer. This is especially useful for secondary command buffers, which can be recorded once and reused multiple times.

```
vkResetCommandBuffer(commandBuffer,
VK_COMMAND_BUFFER_RESET_RELEASE_RESOURCES_BIT);
```

### Command Buffer Pools

Command buffers are allocated from command buffer pools, which are created with vkCreateCommandPool. Command pools manage the memory and reuse of command buffers efficiently.

```
VkCommandPoolCreateInfo poolInfo = {};
poolInfo.sType =
VK_STRUCTURE_TYPE_COMMAND_POOL_CREATE_INFO;
poolInfo.queueFamilyIndex = queueFamilyIndex;
poolInfo.flags =
VK_COMMAND_POOL_CREATE_RESET_COMMAND_BUFFER_BIT; //
Allow resetting of command buffers
```

```
if (vkCreateCommandPool(device, &poolInfo, nullptr,
&commandPool) != VK_SUCCESS) {
    throw std::runtime_error("Failed to create command
pool!");
}
```

## Summary

Vulkan command buffers are vital for issuing rendering and compute commands to the GPU. They provide fine-grained control over the rendering process and enable efficient recording and execution of graphics commands. Understanding how to create, record, and submit command buffers is essential for effective Vulkan graphics programming. In the following sections, we'll delve deeper into graphics pipelines and other aspects of Vulkan graphics programming.

## Section 5.2: Graphics Pipelines in Vulkan

Graphics pipelines in Vulkan are a key component of the rendering process, defining how vertices and fragments are processed to produce the final image. Vulkan allows for a high degree of customization and optimization in graphics pipelines, making it a powerful tool for achieving high-performance graphics rendering. In this section, we'll explore the concept of graphics pipelines in Vulkan. ### Overview of Graphics Pipelines

A graphics pipeline in Vulkan is a series of programmable stages and fixed-function operations that process vertex data and produce a final image. Each stage of the pipeline performs a specific task, and you can customize these stages to suit your rendering needs. The key stages of a typical graphics pipeline include: 1. **Vertex Input:** This stage defines the format of vertex data and how it's fetched from vertex buffers. 2. **Vertex Shader:** The vertex shader processes each vertex's position and attributes, transforming them from object space to screen space. 3. **Tessellation Control Shader (Optional):** If tessellation is used, this stage controls how patches are subdivided. 4. **Tessellation Evaluation Shader (Optional):** This stage computes the final position of tessellated vertices. 5. **Geometry Shader (Optional):** The geometry shader can generate additional vertices or modify existing ones. 6. **Fragment Shader:** The fragment shader calculates the final color and depth of each pixel. 7. **Rasterization:** This stage converts the processed vertices into fragments, which represent the pixels on the screen. 8. **Depth and Stencil Test:** Depth and stencil tests are performed to determine whether fragments are visible. 9. **Blending:** Fragments are blended with the existing framebuffer contents based on blending equations. 10. **Output Merger:** The final pixel values are written to the framebuffer. ### Creating Graphics Pipelines

To create a custom graphics pipeline in Vulkan, you need to specify the pipeline stages and their configuration. This involves creating shader modules for the vertex and fragment shaders, defining the vertex input format, specifying the pipeline layout, and setting other pipeline parameters.

Here's an overview of the steps to create a graphics pipeline: 1. **Shader Modules:** Load and create shader modules for the vertex and fragment shaders. 2. **Vertex Input:** Define the vertex input format, including vertex attributes and bindings. 3. **Pipeline Layout:** Create a pipeline layout that defines the uniform variables and descriptors used by the shaders. 4. **Shader Stages:** Specify the shader stages and their corresponding shader modules. 5. **Rasterization State:** Set rasterization parameters, such as polygon mode, culling, and line width. 6. **Multisampling:** Configure multisampling settings if anti-aliasing is desired. 7. **Depth and Stencil:** Configure depth and stencil testing and state. 8. **Color Blending:** Define color blending parameters for each color attachment. 9. **Viewport and Scissor:** Set viewport and scissor parameters for the rendering region. 10. **Dynamic State (Optional):** Specify any dynamic state parameters that can change without recreating the pipeline. 11. **Create Graphics Pipeline:** Create the graphics pipeline using the specified configuration. ### Pipeline Caching and Reuse

Vulkan provides mechanisms for pipeline caching and reuse, which can significantly improve application performance. Pipeline caching allows you to store compiled pipeline objects and reuse them in subsequent runs, reducing the time spent on pipeline creation.

To enable pipeline caching, you can create a pipeline cache object and pass it when creating pipelines. This cache can be saved to disk and reused across different runs of your application.

```
VkPipelineCacheCreateInfo cacheInfo = {};
cacheInfo.sType =
VK_STRUCTURE_TYPE_PIPELINE_CACHE_CREATE_INFO;

VkPipelineCache pipelineCache;
if (vkCreatePipelineCache(device, &cacheInfo, nullptr,
&pipelineCache) != VK_SUCCESS) {
    throw std::runtime_error("Failed to create pipeline
cache!");
}
```

Summary

Graphics pipelines in Vulkan are a fundamental component of graphics programming, defining how vertices are processed and how fragments are generated. Customizing and optimizing pipelines for specific rendering tasks is essential for achieving high performance in Vulkan applications. Understanding the various stages and configuration options of graphics pipelines is crucial for harnessing the full power of Vulkan's graphics rendering capabilities. In the next section, we'll explore Vulkan render passes, which play a crucial role in defining the structure of rendering operations.

## Section 5.3: Vulkan Render Passes

Vulkan render passes are a fundamental concept for defining the structure of rendering operations and managing framebuffer attachments. Render passes specify which attachments are involved in rendering, the load and store operations for each attachment, and the subpasses that define the rendering stages. In this section, we'll delve into the details of Vulkan render passes. ### Overview of Render Passes

A Vulkan render pass is a description of a series of rendering operations that produce a final image. Render passes provide several benefits, including: - **Efficiency:** Render passes allow Vulkan to optimize memory and cache usage during rendering operations. - **Explicitness:** Render passes explicitly define the structure of rendering, making it easier to understand and debug rendering code. - **Multisampling and Load/Store Operations:** Render passes define how multisampling is performed and how attachment data is loaded and stored. - **Subpasses:** Render passes can consist of multiple subpasses, which can be useful for techniques like deferred rendering. ### Attachment Descriptions

In Vulkan render passes, attachments are the images that are read from or written to during rendering. Each attachment has an associated description that specifies its format, sample count, and how it's used during rendering. Attachment descriptions also define the load and store operations for each attachment at the beginning and end of each subpass.

Here's an example of defining an attachment description:

```
VkAttachmentDescription colorAttachment = {};
colorAttachment.format = swapChainImageFormat;
colorAttachment.samples = VK_SAMPLE_COUNT_1_BIT;
colorAttachment.loadOp = VK_ATTACHMENT_LOAD_OP_CLEAR;
// Clear the attachment at the start of the render pass
colorAttachment.storeOp = VK_ATTACHMENT_STORE_OP_STORE;
// Store the attachment at the end of the render pass
colorAttachment.stencilLoadOp =
VK_ATTACHMENT_LOAD_OP_DONT_CARE;
colorAttachment.stencilStoreOp =
VK_ATTACHMENT_STORE_OP_DONT_CARE;
colorAttachment.initialLayout =
VK_IMAGE_LAYOUT_UNDEFINED;  // Layout before the render
pass
```

```
colorAttachment.finalLayout =
VK_IMAGE_LAYOUT_PRESENT_SRC_KHR;  // Layout after the
render pass
```

## Subpasses

Render passes in Vulkan can consist of multiple subpasses, each of which represents a rendering stage. Subpasses define dependencies between them, making it possible to optimize memory usage and allow for automatic layout transitions of attachments.

Here's an example of defining a subpass:

```
VkSubpassDescription subpass = {};
subpass.pipelineBindPoint =
VK_PIPELINE_BIND_POINT_GRAPHICS; // Subpass type
subpass.colorAttachmentCount = 1; // Number of color
attachments
subpass.pColorAttachments = &colorAttachmentRef; //
Reference to color attachment
subpass.pDepthStencilAttachment = &depthAttachmentRef;
// Reference to depth attachment (if used)
```

### Dependency Between Subpasses

Dependencies between subpasses are crucial for ensuring that rendering operations are performed in the correct order. Dependencies are defined by VkSubpassDependency structures, which specify the source and destination subpasses and the stages at which the dependency occurs.

```
VkSubpassDependency dependency = {};
dependency.srcSubpass = VK_SUBPASS_EXTERNAL; // Special
value for external subpass (before or after render
pass)
dependency.dstSubpass = 0; // Index of the destination
subpass
dependency.srcStageMask =
VK_PIPELINE_STAGE_COLOR_ATTACHMENT_OUTPUT_BIT;
dependency.srcAccessMask = 0;
dependency.dstStageMask =
```

```
VK_PIPELINE_STAGE_COLOR_ATTACHMENT_OUTPUT_BIT;
dependency.dstAccessMask =
VK_ACCESS_COLOR_ATTACHMENT_WRITE_BIT;
```

Creating a Render Pass

To create a Vulkan render pass, you need to specify the attachments, subpasses, and dependencies that define the rendering structure. Once the render pass is created, it can be used when creating graphics pipelines and framebuffers.

```
VkRenderPassCreateInfo renderPassInfo = {};
renderPassInfo.sType =
VK_STRUCTURE_TYPE_RENDER_PASS_CREATE_INFO;
renderPassInfo.attachmentCount = 1; // Number of
attachments
renderPassInfo.pAttachments = &colorAttachment; //
Pointer to attachment descriptions
renderPassInfo.subpassCount = 1; // Number of subpasses
renderPassInfo.pSubpasses = &subpass; // Pointer to
subpasses
renderPassInfo.dependencyCount = 1; // Number of
dependencies
renderPassInfo.pDependencies = &dependency; // Pointer
to dependencies

VkRenderPass renderPass;
if (vkCreateRenderPass(device, &renderPassInfo,
nullptr, &renderPass) != VK_SUCCESS) {
    throw std::runtime_error("Failed to create render
pass!");
}
```

Using Render Passes

Once a Vulkan render pass is created, it can be used when creating framebuffers and graphics pipelines. Framebuffers specify the attachments used during rendering, and graphics pipelines reference the render pass to determine how rendering operations are structured.

Render passes in Vulkan provide fine-grained control over rendering operations, allowing for efficient memory usage, explicit definition of attachment usage, and optimization of rendering dependencies. Understanding how to create and use render passes is crucial for building efficient Vulkan applications. In the following sections, we'll explore additional aspects of Vulkan graphics programming.

## Section 5.4: Uniform Buffers and Push Constants

Uniform buffers and push constants are mechanisms in Vulkan that allow you to pass data to shaders from your application. These mechanisms are crucial for sending dynamic data like transformation matrices, lighting information, and other per-frame or per-object data to the GPU shaders. In this section, we'll explore uniform buffers and push constants in Vulkan. ### Uniform Buffers

Uniform buffers are a way to send data to shaders in a Vulkan application. They are often used for data that changes between draw calls, such as model-view-projection matrices, light positions, or material properties. Here's how you can set up and use a uniform buffer: 1. **Create a Buffer:** First, create a buffer in Vulkan to hold your uniform data. This buffer is typically backed by GPU memory.

```
VkBufferCreateInfo bufferInfo = {};
bufferInfo.sType =
VK_STRUCTURE_TYPE_BUFFER_CREATE_INFO;
bufferInfo.size = sizeof(UniformBufferObject);
bufferInfo.usage = VK_BUFFER_USAGE_UNIFORM_BUFFER_BIT;
bufferInfo.sharingMode = VK_SHARING_MODE_EXCLUSIVE;

if (vkCreateBuffer(device, &bufferInfo, nullptr,
&uniformBuffer) != VK_SUCCESS) {
    throw std::runtime_error("Failed to create uniform
buffer!");
}
```

1.  **Allocate and Bind Memory:** Allocate memory for the buffer and bind it to the buffer. Then, copy your uniform data to this memory.

```
VkMemoryRequirements memRequirements;
vkGetBufferMemoryRequirements(device, uniformBuffer,
&memRequirements);

VkMemoryAllocateInfo allocInfo = {};
allocInfo.sType =
VK_STRUCTURE_TYPE_MEMORY_ALLOCATE_INFO;
allocInfo.allocationSize = memRequirements.size;
allocInfo.memoryTypeIndex =
findMemoryType(memRequirements.memoryTypeBits,
VK_MEMORY_PROPERTY_HOST_VISIBLE_BIT |
VK_MEMORY_PROPERTY_HOST_COHERENT_BIT);

if (vkAllocateMemory(device, &allocInfo, nullptr,
&uniformBufferMemory) != VK_SUCCESS) {
    throw std::runtime_error("Failed to allocate
uniform buffer memory!");
}

vkBindBufferMemory(device, uniformBuffer,
uniformBufferMemory, 0);

void* data;
vkMapMemory(device, uniformBufferMemory, 0,
sizeof(UniformBufferObject), 0, &data);
memcpy(data, &ubo, sizeof(UniformBufferObject));
vkUnmapMemory(device, uniformBufferMemory);
```

1.  **Binding the Uniform Buffer:** In your shader code, you declare a uniform buffer and its layout.

```
layout(set = 0, binding = 0) buffer UniformBufferObject
{
    mat4 model;
    mat4 view;
    mat4 projection;
} ubo;
```

1. **Updating Uniform Data:** Whenever your uniform data changes (e.g., in a new frame), you need to update the uniform buffer's memory. ### Push Constants

Push constants are another way to send data to shaders, but they are more limited in size and scope compared to uniform buffers. Push constants are typically used for small amounts of frequently changing data, such as material properties, transformation matrices, or shader parameters. Here's how to use push constants: 1. **Define Push Constants:** In your shader code, you declare a push constant block and its layout.

```
layout(push_constant) uniform PushConstants {
    vec4 color;
    float intensity;
} pushConstants;
```

1. **Specify Push Constants in Pipeline Layout:** When creating your graphics pipeline, specify the push constant range in the pipeline layout.

```
VkPushConstantRange pushConstantRange = {};
pushConstantRange.stageFlags =
VK_SHADER_STAGE_VERTEX_BIT; // Specify the shader stage
that uses push constants
pushConstantRange.offset = 0; // Offset in bytes from
the start of push constants
pushConstantRange.size = sizeof(PushConstants); // Size
of push constants

VkPipelineLayoutCreateInfo pipelineLayoutInfo = {};
pipelineLayoutInfo.sType =
VK_STRUCTURE_TYPE_PIPELINE_LAYOUT_CREATE_INFO;
pipelineLayoutInfo.pushConstantRangeCount = 1;
pipelineLayoutInfo.pPushConstantRanges =
&pushConstantRange;

if (vkCreatePipelineLayout(device, &pipelineLayoutInfo,
nullptr, &pipelineLayout) != VK_SUCCESS) {
    throw std::runtime_error("Failed to create pipeline
layout!");
}
```

1.  **Updating Push Constants:** When you bind a pipeline and push constants, you can update the push constants with new data before each draw call.

```
PushConstants pushData;
pushData.color = glm::vec4(1.0f, 0.0f, 0.0f, 1.0f);
pushData.intensity = 0.8f;
vkCmdPushConstants(commandBuffer, pipelineLayout,
VK_SHADER_STAGE_VERTEX_BIT, 0, sizeof(PushConstants),
&pushData);
```

Uniform buffers and push constants provide flexible ways to send data to shaders in Vulkan applications. The choice between them depends on the amount and frequency of data updates. Uniform buffers are suitable for larger amounts of data that change less frequently, while push constants are ideal for small, frequently changing data. Understanding when and how to use these mechanisms is essential for efficient Vulkan graphics programming.

## Section 5.5: Vertex Input and Vertex Shaders in Vulkan

In Vulkan graphics programming, understanding how to define vertex input and use vertex shaders is fundamental to rendering 3D objects efficiently. This section explores the concepts of vertex input and vertex shaders in Vulkan. ### Vertex Input

Vertex input defines the format of vertex data that is sent to the graphics pipeline. It includes information about vertex attributes, such as position, color, texture coordinates, and normals. Properly defining vertex input is essential to ensure that the GPU processes vertex data correctly.

To set up vertex input in Vulkan, you need to: 1. **Define Vertex Attributes:** Create a structure that represents the vertex data format. This structure should include members corresponding to the vertex attributes, along with their formats and offsets.

```
struct Vertex {
    glm::vec3 position;
    glm::vec3 color;
```

```cpp
    glm::vec2 texCoord;

    static VkVertexInputBindingDescription
getBindingDescription() {
        // Define how data for a single vertex is
stored
    }

    static
std::vector<VkVertexInputAttributeDescription>
getAttributeDescriptions() {
        // Describe the vertex attributes and their
format
    }
};
```

1. **Binding Description:** Define how the vertex data is arranged in memory. This includes the stride (size of a single vertex) and whether the data advances after each vertex or instance.

2. **Attribute Descriptions:** Specify the attributes and their formats, offsets, and binding points. These descriptions must match the definitions in the vertex shader.

3. **Pipeline Layout:** Ensure that the pipeline layout references the vertex input format. ### Vertex Shaders

Vertex shaders in Vulkan are responsible for processing individual vertices in the graphics pipeline. They transform vertex positions from object space to screen space and may perform other tasks like lighting calculations. To use vertex shaders effectively: 1. **Create a Vertex Shader Module:** First, compile your vertex shader code and create a shader module.

```cpp
VkShaderModule createShaderModule(const
std::vector<char>& code) {
        // Load the shader code and create a shader module
}
```

1. **Specify Shader Stages:** When creating the graphics pipeline, specify the vertex shader module and its stage.

```
VkPipelineShaderStageCreateInfo vertexShaderStageInfo =
{};
vertexShaderStageInfo.sType =
VK_STRUCTURE_TYPE_PIPELINE_SHADER_STAGE_CREATE_INFO;
vertexShaderStageInfo.stage =
VK_SHADER_STAGE_VERTEX_BIT;
vertexShaderStageInfo.module = vertexShaderModule;
vertexShaderStageInfo.pName = "main"; // Entry point in
the shader code
```

1. **Define Vertex Shader Code:** In your shader code,
   implement the main function to process each vertex. This
   function typically transforms the vertex position and may
   perform other operations.

```
#version 450

layout(location = 0) in vec3 inPosition;
layout(location = 1) in vec3 inColor;
layout(location = 2) in vec2 inTexCoord;


layout(location = 0) out vec3 fragColor;
layout(location = 1) out vec2 fragTexCoord;


layout(push_constant) uniform PushConstants {
    mat4 model;
    mat4 view;
    mat4 projection;
} pushConstants;

void main() {
    // Transform vertex position using model-view-
projection matrices
    vec4 modelViewProjPos = pushConstants.projection *
pushConstants.view * pushConstants.model *
vec4(inPosition, 1.0);
    gl_Position = modelViewProjPos;

    // Pass other vertex attributes to the fragment
shader
    fragColor = inColor;
```

```
    fragTexCoord = inTexCoord;
}
```

Vertex shaders play a crucial role in the rendering process, and they can be customized to implement various rendering techniques. Properly defining vertex input and implementing vertex shaders is essential for rendering 3D objects accurately in Vulkan applications.

In the next sections, we'll explore more advanced topics in Vulkan graphics programming, including lighting, texturing, and optimizations for improved performance.

# Chapter 6: Memory Management in Vulkan

## Section 6.1: Vulkan Memory Allocation

Memory management is a critical aspect of Vulkan graphics programming, and understanding how memory is allocated and used is essential for efficient rendering. Vulkan provides explicit memory management control, which allows you to allocate and manage memory resources according to your application's specific needs. In this section, we'll explore Vulkan's memory allocation mechanisms. ### Memory Types and Properties

Vulkan distinguishes between different memory types, each with specific properties, to cater to various resource requirements. These properties include: - **VK_MEMORY_PROPERTY_DEVICE_LOCAL_BIT:** Memory that is local to the GPU, ideal for large, long-lived resources like textures and vertex buffers. - **VK_MEMORY_PROPERTY_HOST_VISIBLE_BIT:** Memory that can be mapped by the CPU for data transfers between CPU and GPU. - **VK_MEMORY_PROPERTY_HOST_COHERENT_BIT:** Memory that ensures CPU writes are immediately visible to the GPU. - **VK_MEMORY_PROPERTY_HOST_CACHED_BIT:** Memory that is cached on the CPU side, which can improve readback performance. -

**VK_MEMORY_PROPERTY_LAZILY_ALLOCATED_BIT:** Memory that is allocated only when it is used, suitable for resources that are not frequently accessed. ### Memory Allocation with Vulkan

To allocate memory in Vulkan, you need to follow these steps: 1. **Query Memory Requirements:** First, determine the memory requirements for the resource you want to allocate using vkGetBufferMemoryRequirements or vkGetImageMemoryRequirements. This provides information about the size, alignment, and memory type requirements.

```
VkMemoryRequirements memRequirements;
vkGetBufferMemoryRequirements(device, buffer,
&memRequirements);
```

1. **Select Suitable Memory Type:** Vulkan allows you to select a memory type that meets the requirements of the resource and your application. You can query the memory properties supported by each memory type.

```
uint32_t findMemoryType(uint32_t typeFilter,
VkMemoryPropertyFlags properties) {
    for (uint32_t i = 0; i <
memoryProperties.memoryTypeCount; i++) {
        if ((typeFilter & (1 << i)) &&
(memoryProperties.memoryTypes[i].propertyFlags &
properties) == properties) {
            return i;
        }
    }
    throw std::runtime_error("Failed to find suitable
memory type!");
}
```

1. **Allocate Memory:** Once you've identified a suitable memory type, you can allocate memory using vkAllocateMemory.

```
VkMemoryAllocateInfo allocInfo = {};
allocInfo.sType =
VK_STRUCTURE_TYPE_MEMORY_ALLOCATE_INFO;
allocInfo.allocationSize = memRequirements.size;
allocInfo.memoryTypeIndex =
```

```
findMemoryType(memRequirements.memoryTypeBits,
VK_MEMORY_PROPERTY_HOST_VISIBLE_BIT);

if (vkAllocateMemory(device, &allocInfo, nullptr,
&bufferMemory) != VK_SUCCESS) {
    throw std::runtime_error("Failed to allocate buffer
memory!");
}
```

1. **Bind Memory:** After successfully allocating memory,
   bind it to the resource (buffer or image) using
   vkBindBufferMemory or vkBindImageMemory.

```
vkBindBufferMemory(device, buffer, bufferMemory, 0);
```

1. **Map and Unmap Memory:** For memory types with
   VK_MEMORY_PROPERTY_HOST_VISIBLE_BIT, you can map
   the memory to your application's address space,
   manipulate the data, and then unmap it. This allows for
   efficient data transfers between CPU and GPU.

```
void* data;
vkMapMemory(device, bufferMemory, 0, size, 0, &data);
// Modify data here
vkUnmapMemory(device, bufferMemory);
```

1. **Free Memory:** When you're done using the allocated
   memory, don't forget to free it using vkFreeMemory.

```
vkFreeMemory(device, bufferMemory, nullptr);
```

Proper memory management in Vulkan is crucial for optimizing
your application's performance and ensuring efficient resource
utilization. Understanding memory types and properties,
selecting appropriate memory types, and using memory
allocation functions correctly are essential steps in Vulkan
memory management.

## Section 6.2: Vulkan Buffers and Images

In Vulkan graphics programming, buffers and images are
fundamental objects used to store and manage data. Buffers are
typically used for storing raw data, such as vertex and index

data, while images are used for textures and framebuffers. This section explores how to create and manage buffers and images in Vulkan. ### Vulkan Buffers

Buffers in Vulkan are used to store raw data, and they come in several types, including vertex buffers, index buffers, uniform buffers, and storage buffers. To create a buffer in Vulkan, you need to follow these steps: 1. **Buffer Creation:** Create a VkBuffer object that represents the buffer. You specify the size and usage flags for the buffer.

```
VkBufferCreateInfo bufferInfo = {};
bufferInfo.sType =
VK_STRUCTURE_TYPE_BUFFER_CREATE_INFO;
bufferInfo.size = bufferSize;
bufferInfo.usage = VK_BUFFER_USAGE_VERTEX_BUFFER_BIT;
bufferInfo.sharingMode = VK_SHARING_MODE_EXCLUSIVE; //
Can be shared among multiple queues

VkBuffer vertexBuffer;
if (vkCreateBuffer(device, &bufferInfo, nullptr,
&vertexBuffer) != VK_SUCCESS) {
    throw std::runtime_error("Failed to create vertex
buffer!");
}
```

1.  **Allocate Memory:** After creating the buffer, you need to allocate memory for it. This involves determining the memory requirements and selecting an appropriate memory type, as discussed in the previous section (6.1).
2.  **Bind Buffer to Memory:** Once you have allocated memory, bind the buffer to that memory.

```
vkBindBufferMemory(device, vertexBuffer,
vertexBufferMemory, 0);
```

1.  **Copying Data to Buffers:** To populate the buffer with data, you can use the Vulkan memory mapping mechanism. Map the buffer memory, copy data into it, and then unmap the memory.

```
void* data;
vkMapMemory(device, vertexBufferMemory, 0, bufferSize,
0, &data);
memcpy(data, vertices.data(), (size_t)bufferSize);
vkUnmapMemory(device, vertexBufferMemory);
```

Vulkan Images

Images in Vulkan are used to store texture data and
framebuffers. Creating an image involves several steps: 1. **Image
Creation:** Create a `VkImage` object that represents the image.
You specify the image's type, format, extent (dimensions), usage
flags, and other parameters.

```
VkImageCreateInfo imageInfo = {};
imageInfo.sType = VK_STRUCTURE_TYPE_IMAGE_CREATE_INFO;
imageInfo.imageType = VK_IMAGE_TYPE_2D;
imageInfo.extent.width = texWidth;
imageInfo.extent.height = texHeight;
imageInfo.extent.depth = 1;
imageInfo.mipLevels = 1;
imageInfo.arrayLayers = 1;
imageInfo.format = VK_FORMAT_R8G8B8A8_SRGB;
imageInfo.tiling = VK_IMAGE_TILING_OPTIMAL;
imageInfo.initialLayout = VK_IMAGE_LAYOUT_UNDEFINED;
imageInfo.usage = VK_IMAGE_USAGE_TRANSFER_DST_BIT |
VK_IMAGE_USAGE_SAMPLED_BIT;
imageInfo.samples = VK_SAMPLE_COUNT_1_BIT;
imageInfo.sharingMode = VK_SHARING_MODE_EXCLUSIVE;
```

1.  **Allocate Memory for Images:** Similar to buffers, you
    need to allocate memory for images, considering their
    requirements. Select an appropriate memory type and
    bind the image to that memory.
2.  **Transition Image Layout:** Images in Vulkan have layout
    transitions to specify how they are used (e.g., transferring
    from `VK_IMAGE_LAYOUT_UNDEFINED` to
    `VK_IMAGE_LAYOUT_TRANSFER_DST_OPTIMAL`).

```
transitionImageLayout(image, VK_FORMAT_R8G8B8A8_SRGB,
VK_IMAGE_LAYOUT_UNDEFINED,
VK_IMAGE_LAYOUT_TRANSFER_DST_OPTIMAL);
```

1. **Copying Data to Images:** To populate an image with data, you can use the vkCmdCopyBufferToImage command within a command buffer.

```
VkBufferImageCopy region = {};
region.bufferOffset = 0;
region.bufferRowLength = 0;
region.bufferImageHeight = 0;
region.imageSubresource.aspectMask =
VK_IMAGE_ASPECT_COLOR_BIT;
region.imageSubresource.mipLevel = 0;
region.imageSubresource.baseArrayLayer = 0;
region.imageSubresource.layerCount = 1;
region.imageOffset = {0, 0, 0};
region.imageExtent = {texWidth, texHeight, 1};


vkCmdCopyBufferToImage(commandBuffer, buffer, image,
VK_IMAGE_LAYOUT_TRANSFER_DST_OPTIMAL, 1, &region);
```

1. **Transition Image Layout Again:** After copying data to the image, transition its layout to its final usage, such as VK_IMAGE_LAYOUT_SHADER_READ_ONLY_OPTIMAL for texture access.

```
transitionImageLayout(image, VK_FORMAT_R8G8B8A8_SRGB,
VK_IMAGE_LAYOUT_TRANSFER_DST_OPTIMAL,
VK_IMAGE_LAYOUT_SHADER_READ_ONLY_OPTIMAL);
```

Vulkan buffers and images are versatile tools for managing data in graphics applications. Properly creating, allocating, and managing these resources is essential for efficient rendering and achieving the desired graphical results.

## Section 6.3: Managing Memory in Vulkan

Efficient memory management is a crucial aspect of Vulkan graphics programming. In addition to allocating memory for buffers and images, you also need to manage that memory effectively to ensure optimal performance and resource utilization. This section explores various techniques for managing memory in Vulkan. ### Memory Pools

Vulkan allows you to create memory pools to efficiently allocate and manage memory for multiple resources of the same type. Instead of allocating memory individually for each buffer or image, you can allocate a chunk of memory from a pool and use it for multiple resources.

To create a memory pool, you need to specify the memory type, size, and allocation flags. Then, you can allocate memory from this pool for your resources.

```
VkMemoryPoolCreateInfo poolInfo = {};
poolInfo.sType =
VK_STRUCTURE_TYPE_MEMORY_POOL_CREATE_INFO;
poolInfo.memoryTypeIndex = memoryTypeIndex;
poolInfo.blockSize = blockSize;
poolInfo.flags =
VK_MEMORY_POOL_CREATE_RESET_COMMAND_BUFFER_BIT;

VkMemoryPool memoryPool;
if (vkCreateMemoryPool(device, &poolInfo, nullptr,
&memoryPool) != VK_SUCCESS) {
    throw std::runtime_error("Failed to create memory
pool!");
}
```

Suballocations

Within a memory pool, you can perform suballocations to divide the allocated memory into smaller chunks for individual resources. Suballocations enable efficient utilization of memory by minimizing fragmentation and preventing memory waste.

```
VkMemoryPoolAllocateInfo allocateInfo = {};
allocateInfo.sType =
VK_STRUCTURE_TYPE_MEMORY_POOL_ALLOCATE_INFO;
allocateInfo.pool = memoryPool;
allocateInfo.size = allocationSize;

VkDeviceMemory deviceMemory;
if (vkAllocateMemoryFromPool(device, &allocateInfo,
nullptr, &deviceMemory) != VK_SUCCESS) {
```

```
    throw std::runtime_error("Failed to allocate memory
from pool!");
}
```

## Memory Management Best Practices

When managing memory in Vulkan, it's essential to follow these
best practices: 1. **Reuse Memory:** Reuse allocated memory
whenever possible. Instead of allocating new memory for each
resource, consider reusing memory that is no longer needed by
releasing it from one resource and allocating it for another. 2.
**Memory Barriers and Synchronization:** Properly use memory
barriers and synchronization to ensure that memory writes and
reads are properly ordered between CPU and GPU operations.
This is crucial to avoid data corruption and synchronization
issues. 3. **Free Unused Memory:** Periodically check and release
memory that is no longer in use. Vulkan provides mechanisms to
free and release memory to the system when it's no longer
needed. 4. **Allocate Memory Based on Resource Lifetimes:**
Allocate memory based on the expected lifetime of the resource.
Short-lived resources can use transient memory, while long-
lived resources can use dedicated memory. 5. **Memory
Budgeting:** Keep track of memory usage and budgeting to avoid
running out of memory during runtime. Vulkan provides tools
and extensions to query available memory and manage memory
budgets effectively. 6. **Use Dedicated Allocation Libraries:**
Consider using dedicated memory allocation libraries like
Vulkan Memory Allocator (VMA) to simplify memory
management and improve memory allocation efficiency.

Proper memory management in Vulkan is essential for building
high-performance graphics applications. By utilizing memory
pools, performing suballocations, and following best practices,
you can optimize memory usage and achieve better overall
performance in your Vulkan applications.

## Section 6.4: Memory Barriers and Synchronization

In Vulkan graphics programming, memory barriers and
synchronization are essential for ensuring that memory reads

and writes are correctly ordered between different operations, including those executed on the CPU and GPU. Memory barriers help prevent data hazards and synchronization issues that can lead to visual artifacts and incorrect rendering. This section dives into memory barriers and synchronization in Vulkan. ### Memory Barriers

Memory barriers define a point in the execution of a command buffer where memory dependencies must be enforced. They ensure that previous memory writes are visible to subsequent memory reads. Vulkan provides different types of memory barriers, including: - **VK_ACCESS_MEMORY_READ_BIT:** Denotes a memory read operation. - **VK_ACCESS_MEMORY_WRITE_BIT:** Denotes a memory write operation. - **VK_ACCESS_MEMORY_READ_BIT | VK_ACCESS_MEMORY_WRITE_BIT:** Denotes both read and write operations. - **VK_ACCESS_HOST_READ_BIT:** Denotes a host (CPU) read operation. - **VK_ACCESS_HOST_WRITE_BIT:** Denotes a host (CPU) write operation. - **VK_ACCESS_TRANSFER_READ_BIT:** Denotes a transfer read operation. - **VK_ACCESS_TRANSFER_WRITE_BIT:** Denotes a transfer write operation.

Memory barriers are typically used in scenarios like: 1. **Transitioning Image Layouts:** When transitioning an image from one layout to another (e.g., from VK_IMAGE_LAYOUT_COLOR_ATTACHMENT_OPTIMAL to VK_IMAGE_LAYOUT_SHADER_READ_ONLY_OPTIMAL), memory barriers ensure that the previous layout's writes are visible to subsequent reads.

```
VkImageMemoryBarrier barrier = {};
barrier.sType = VK_STRUCTURE_TYPE_IMAGE_MEMORY_BARRIER;
barrier.srcAccessMask =
VK_ACCESS_COLOR_ATTACHMENT_WRITE_BIT;
barrier.dstAccessMask = VK_ACCESS_SHADER_READ_BIT;
barrier.oldLayout =
VK_IMAGE_LAYOUT_COLOR_ATTACHMENT_OPTIMAL;
barrier.newLayout =
VK_IMAGE_LAYOUT_SHADER_READ_ONLY_OPTIMAL;
```

```
// ...
vkCmdPipelineBarrier(commandBuffer, ...);
```

1. **Synchronization Between Command Buffers:** Memory
   barriers can synchronize access to resources between
   different command buffers. For example, ensuring that a
   resource is fully written to by one command buffer before
   it's read by another. ### Pipeline Barriers

Pipeline barriers are more general synchronization primitives
that encompass memory barriers. They allow synchronization
between different pipeline stages and can include both memory
and execution dependencies. Pipeline barriers are specified
using the vkCmdPipelineBarrier function and can synchronize
multiple aspects of GPU operations, including graphics, compute,
and transfer commands.

```
vkCmdPipelineBarrier(
    commandBuffer,
    VK_PIPELINE_STAGE_TOP_OF_PIPE_BIT,
    VK_PIPELINE_STAGE_BOTTOM_OF_PIPE_BIT,
    0,
    0, nullptr,
    0, nullptr,
    1, &barrier
);
```

Semaphore and Fence Synchronization

Vulkan also provides semaphores and fences for synchronization
between command buffers and queues. Semaphores are used for
synchronization within a single queue, while fences are used for
synchronization between queues or between the CPU and GPU.
They ensure that certain operations are completed before others
are started.

```
// Semaphore usage
VkSemaphoreCreateInfo semaphoreInfo = {};
semaphoreInfo.sType =
VK_STRUCTURE_TYPE_SEMAPHORE_CREATE_INFO;
VkSemaphore semaphore;
```

```
vkCreateSemaphore(device, &semaphoreInfo, nullptr,
&semaphore);

// Fence usage
VkFenceCreateInfo fenceInfo = {};
fenceInfo.sType = VK_STRUCTURE_TYPE_FENCE_CREATE_INFO;
fenceInfo.flags = VK_FENCE_CREATE_SIGNALED_BIT; //
Optionally start signaled
VkFence fence;
vkCreateFence(device, &fenceInfo, nullptr, &fence);
```

In Vulkan, careful use of memory barriers, pipeline barriers, semaphores, and fences is crucial to achieving correct and efficient synchronization between GPU and CPU operations. Understanding when and how to apply these synchronization primitives is essential for building robust and performant Vulkan applications.

## Section 6.5: Debugging Memory Issues

Debugging memory-related issues is a critical aspect of graphics programming in Vulkan. Mishandling memory can lead to various problems, including crashes, memory leaks, and incorrect rendering. This section covers common memory-related issues in Vulkan and provides tips on how to debug and prevent them. ### Memory Leaks

Memory leaks occur when allocated memory is not properly released, causing your application to consume more and more memory over time. Vulkan resources, such as buffers, images, and memory allocations, should be released when they are no longer needed. Failing to do so can lead to memory leaks.

To detect memory leaks, you can use debugging tools and validation layers provided by Vulkan. These tools can report unreleased resources and memory leaks during application runtime. ### Resource Lifetime Mismatch

Resource lifetime mismatches can occur when you attempt to use a Vulkan resource that has already been destroyed or freed. This can lead to crashes or incorrect rendering.

To prevent resource lifetime mismatches, ensure that you: - Properly manage the lifetime of Vulkan resources by destroying them when they are no longer needed. - Avoid using resources that have already been destroyed or freed. ### Invalid Memory Access

Invalid memory access can result from reading or writing memory that has not been properly allocated or is out of bounds. It can lead to crashes or undefined behavior.

To prevent invalid memory access: - Always allocate memory for Vulkan resources before using them. - Ensure that you provide correct buffer and image sizes and offsets. - Use memory barriers and synchronization to ensure memory accesses are correctly ordered. ### Using Freed Memory

Using memory that has been freed can lead to crashes and undefined behavior. Vulkan does not automatically invalidate pointers to memory that has been released.

To avoid using freed memory: - Set Vulkan resource handles to null or invalid values after they have been destroyed. - Avoid accessing resources that have been released. ### Debugging Tools and Validation Layers

Vulkan provides validation layers that can help you detect and debug memory-related issues during development. Enabling validation layers when creating the Vulkan instance can provide valuable error messages and warnings related to memory management.

Additionally, you can use external memory analysis tools and profilers to identify memory-related problems in your Vulkan application. These tools can help you track memory allocations and deallocations and identify potential memory leaks. ### Proper Error Handling

Implement robust error handling in your Vulkan application. Check the return values of Vulkan functions for errors and handle them appropriately. When an error occurs, make sure to release any allocated resources and provide clear error messages to aid in debugging.

In summary, debugging memory issues is a critical part of Vulkan graphics programming. By following best practices for resource management, enabling validation layers, using external tools, and implementing proper error handling, you can minimize memory-related problems and ensure the stability and correctness of your Vulkan applications.

# Chapter 7: Vulkan Rendering Techniques

## Section 7.1: Multi-Pass Rendering in Vulkan

Multi-pass rendering is a technique commonly used in computer graphics to achieve complex visual effects that require multiple stages of rendering. In Vulkan, multi-pass rendering involves rendering an object or scene in multiple passes, with each pass applying different shaders, materials, or post-processing effects. This section explores multi-pass rendering techniques in Vulkan. ### The Concept of Multi-Pass Rendering

Multi-pass rendering involves breaking down the rendering process into several stages or passes, each of which contributes to the final rendered image. These passes can perform various tasks, such as applying different lighting models, shadows, reflections, and post-processing effects.

The primary reasons for using multi-pass rendering include: 1. **Complex Visual Effects:** Multi-pass rendering allows you to implement advanced visual effects that require multiple rendering stages, such as reflections, refractions, and screen-space effects like motion blur and depth of field. 2. **Efficiency:** By separating rendering into passes, you can optimize each pass for specific tasks. For example, shadow mapping can be performed

in one pass, while lighting calculations are performed in another.
3. **Flexibility:** Multi-pass rendering provides flexibility in creating custom rendering pipelines tailored to your specific application's needs. You can add or remove passes as required.

### Implementing Multi-Pass Rendering in Vulkan

To implement multi-pass rendering in Vulkan, you typically follow these steps: 1. **Create Multiple Render Passes:** Define multiple render passes, each with its set of attachments and subpasses. Each subpass can have its set of shaders and pipeline configurations. 2. **Define Dependencies:** Specify dependencies between render passes to ensure correct order and synchronization between them. Dependencies ensure that data produced in one pass is available for consumption in subsequent passes. 3. **Execute Render Passes:** For each frame, execute the defined render passes in the desired order. This involves binding the appropriate pipelines, shaders, and descriptor sets for each pass and executing command buffers. 4. **Read and Write to Attachments:** Within each pass, read from and write to attachments (e.g., framebuffers and images) as needed. These attachments can store intermediate results or be used for post-processing. 5. **Synchronization and Barriers:** Properly use synchronization primitives like memory barriers and pipeline barriers to ensure memory access and execution order correctness between passes. ### Common Use Cases

Multi-pass rendering is used in various graphics applications for achieving different effects: 1. **Deferred Rendering:** Deferred rendering is a classic example of multi-pass rendering. It involves rendering geometry information into a G-buffer (geometry buffer) in one pass and then performing lighting calculations in subsequent passes using the G-buffer data. 2. **Shadow Mapping:** Shadow mapping often requires multiple passes, including rendering the shadow map and then applying shadow calculations to the scene. 3. **Post-Processing Effects:** Effects like bloom, depth of field, and motion blur are implemented as post-processing passes in a multi-pass rendering pipeline. 4. **Screen-Space Reflections:** To achieve realistic screen-space reflections, multiple passes are used to trace rays and calculate reflections. 5. **Complex Materials:** Some materials, such as those with subsurface scattering or anisotropic properties, may require multi-pass techniques for accurate rendering.

In conclusion, multi-pass rendering in Vulkan enables the creation of visually complex and realistic scenes by breaking down rendering into multiple stages. By properly defining dependencies, handling synchronization, and using Vulkan's capabilities, you can implement advanced graphics effects and achieve high-quality rendering in your Vulkan applications.

## Section 7.2: Deferred Rendering

Deferred rendering is a rendering technique widely used in computer graphics to efficiently handle complex scenes with multiple lights and materials. It offers advantages over traditional forward rendering by decoupling the rendering of geometry from lighting calculations, making it particularly useful for scenarios with many dynamic lights. This section explores the concept of deferred rendering and its implementation in Vulkan. ### Understanding Deferred Rendering

In deferred rendering, the rendering process is split into two major phases: 1. **Geometry Pass:** In this initial pass, the geometry of the scene is rendered into a set of intermediate buffers known as the G-buffer. The G-buffer stores information like position, normal, albedo, and material properties for each pixel in the scene. 2. **Lighting Pass:** After the geometry pass, lighting calculations are performed in a separate pass. This pass uses the information stored in the G-buffer to apply various lighting models and calculate the final pixel color. ### Advantages of Deferred Rendering

Deferred rendering offers several advantages: 1. **Efficiency with Multiple Lights:** Deferred rendering is efficient when dealing with scenes that have many dynamic lights because lighting calculations are performed only for visible pixels in the G-buffer, not for all objects in the scene. 2. **Complex Materials:** Deferred rendering allows for complex material shaders and various material properties to be easily incorporated into the rendering process. 3. **Post-Processing Effects:** Since deferred rendering separates geometry and lighting, it's straightforward to add post-processing effects like bloom, depth of field, and motion blur. ### Implementing Deferred Rendering in Vulkan

To implement deferred rendering in Vulkan, you need to follow these steps: 1. **Create G-Buffer:** Define the G-buffer, which consists of multiple attachments (textures) to store position, normal, albedo, and other relevant information. Create a framebuffer that links these attachments. 2. **Geometry Pass:** In this pass, render the scene's geometry into the G-buffer attachments using appropriate shaders. Bind the framebuffer and render pass for the geometry pass. 3. **Lighting Pass:** In a separate pass, calculate lighting for each pixel using the information stored in the G-buffer. Typically, this involves rendering a fullscreen quad and applying lighting calculations in fragment shaders. The output is accumulated in a final color attachment. 4. **Post-Processing:** Optionally, you can apply post-processing effects in additional passes by using the final color attachment from the lighting pass. 5. **Final Composite:** Finally, composite the results of the lighting pass and any post-processing effects to produce the final image. ### Challenges of Deferred Rendering

While deferred rendering offers many advantages, it also presents some challenges: 1. **Memory Consumption:** Deferred rendering requires storage for the G-buffer, which can be memory-intensive, especially at high resolutions. 2. **Limited Transparency Support:** Handling transparent objects in deferred rendering can be complex and may require additional passes. 3. **Order-Dependent Effects:** Effects like transparency, refraction, and order-dependent materials may require workarounds or additional passes.

In conclusion, deferred rendering is a powerful technique for handling scenes with multiple lights and complex materials in Vulkan. It offers efficiency and flexibility, but it also requires careful management of memory and may pose challenges for certain rendering scenarios. Understanding the trade-offs and properly implementing deferred rendering can lead to visually impressive results in Vulkan applications.

## Section 7.3: Shadow Mapping in Vulkan

Shadow mapping is a fundamental technique used in computer graphics to simulate the effects of shadows in 3D scenes. It is widely employed to enhance the realism and immersion of rendered scenes. In Vulkan, implementing shadow mapping involves rendering depth information from the perspective of a light source and then using that information to determine which areas of the scene are in shadow. This section explores the concept of shadow mapping and how it can be implemented in Vulkan. ### Understanding Shadow Mapping

Shadow mapping is based on the concept of depth mapping. It works by rendering the scene from the perspective of a light source and recording the distances of objects from the light source in a depth map or shadow map. The shadow map is essentially a depth buffer that stores the depth values of the objects as seen from the light source.

The key steps in shadow mapping are as follows: 1. **Shadow Map Generation:** Render the scene from the perspective of the light source to create a shadow map. This involves rendering the scene geometry and recording the depth values of the objects relative to the light source. 2. **Shadow Map Comparison:** During the main rendering pass, each pixel in the scene is transformed into the light space (the perspective of the light source) and compared with the corresponding depth value in the shadow map. If the depth value of a pixel in the shadow map is greater (farther from the light source) than the transformed pixel depth, it means that the pixel is in shadow. 3. **Shadow Calculation:** Based on the results of the shadow map comparison, determine whether a pixel is in shadow or in light. This information is used to modulate the final color of the pixel, simulating the presence or absence of shadows. ### Implementing Shadow Mapping in Vulkan

To implement shadow mapping in Vulkan, you need to follow these general steps: 1. **Create Shadow Map:** Define a framebuffer and image to store the shadow map. The depth values in the shadow map represent the distance of objects from the light source. 2. **Light's View and Projection:** Set up the view and projection matrices for the light source. These matrices define the perspective from which the scene is rendered to create the shadow map. 3. **Shadow Map Generation Pass:** Render the scene from the perspective of the light source, capturing depth information in the shadow map. 4. **Main Rendering Pass:** For each pixel in the main rendering pass, transform it into the light space using the light's view and projection matrices. Compare the depth value of the pixel with the depth value in the shadow map to determine shadowing. 5. **Shadow Calculation:** Based on the shadow comparison result, apply shadowing to the pixel's final color. This is typically done using a shadow factor that modulates the pixel's intensity. 6. **Shadow Biasing:** To prevent shadow acne (artifacts caused by precision issues), you may apply a small bias to the depth values during shadow map generation and shadow comparison. ### Challenges and Optimizations

Implementing shadow mapping in Vulkan comes with challenges such as shadow acne, Peter Panning, and light bleeding. Addressing these issues may involve techniques like shadow map filtering, percentage-closer filtering (PCF), and using cascaded shadow maps for directional lights.

In conclusion, shadow mapping is a crucial technique in Vulkan for simulating shadows in 3D scenes. By carefully implementing shadow map generation, comparison, and shadow calculation, you can enhance the realism of your rendered scenes. Understanding the challenges and optimizations associated with shadow mapping is essential for achieving visually pleasing results in Vulkan applications.

## Section 7.4: Particle Systems in Vulkan

Particle systems are a common technique used in computer graphics to simulate various phenomena such as fire, smoke, sparks, rain, and more. They consist of a large number of small, individually controlled entities (particles) that collectively create dynamic and visually appealing effects. In Vulkan, implementing particle systems involves efficiently rendering and animating a large number of particles. This section explores the concept of particle systems in Vulkan and discusses their implementation. ### Understanding Particle Systems

A particle system is composed of several elements: 1. **Particles:** These are the individual entities that make up the system. Each particle has attributes like position, velocity, color, size, and lifetime. 2. **Emitter:** The emitter is responsible for generating new particles and specifying their initial attributes. It defines the position, velocity, and other properties of emitted particles. 3. **Simulation:** Particles evolve over time based on their attributes. For example, they can move according to their velocity, change color, and decrease in size as they age. Physics simulation can also be applied to particles. 4. **Rendering:** Rendering involves drawing particles as points, sprites, or other shapes. Each particle's position, size, and color are used to generate the final visual output. ### Implementing Particle Systems in Vulkan

Implementing a particle system in Vulkan involves the following steps: 1. **Particle Data:** Define data structures to represent individual particles. This includes attributes like position, velocity, color, size, and lifetime. 2. **Emitter Setup:** Create an emitter that generates new particles at specified intervals and assigns initial attributes. This may involve randomization to create natural-looking particle behavior. 3. **Simulation:** Update the attributes of existing particles over time. This includes integrating particle positions based on their velocity, aging particles, and possibly applying forces or collision detection. 4. **Rendering:** Render the particles using Vulkan's rendering capabilities. This may involve using point sprites, instancing, or other techniques to efficiently draw a large number of particles.

**5. Optimizations:** Implement optimizations to handle a large number of particles efficiently. Techniques like spatial partitioning, sorting particles for efficient rendering, and using GPU instancing can significantly improve performance. **6. Interaction:** If needed, implement interaction between particles and other objects in the scene, such as collision detection and response. **7. Resource Management:** Properly manage resources like vertex buffers, textures, and shaders used for rendering particles. ### Challenges and Considerations

When working with particle systems in Vulkan, you may encounter challenges such as performance optimization, blending modes for rendering, handling transparency, and synchronization between CPU and GPU. Additionally, managing a large number of dynamically created particles and avoiding memory fragmentation are crucial for efficient particle system implementations.

Particle systems can be used for a wide range of effects, including fire, smoke, rain, snow, explosions, and more. The flexibility and versatility of particle systems make them an essential tool for creating dynamic and visually engaging scenes in Vulkan applications.

In conclusion, implementing particle systems in Vulkan allows for the creation of realistic and dynamic visual effects. By carefully managing particle data, simulation, rendering, and optimizations, you can achieve impressive and efficient particle-based graphics in your Vulkan applications.

## Section 7.5: Post-Processing Effects

Post-processing effects are a powerful tool in computer graphics for enhancing the visual quality and realism of rendered scenes. These effects are applied to the final image after the standard rendering pipeline is complete, allowing for various adjustments and enhancements. In Vulkan, post-processing effects can be implemented by using framebuffers, shaders, and rendering passes. This section explores the concept of post-processing

effects and how to implement them in Vulkan. ###
Understanding Post-Processing Effects

Post-processing effects are applied as a series of image
operations on the rendered scene. These operations can include:
1. **Color Grading:** Adjusting the color and tone of the image to
achieve a specific look or mood. 2. **Bloom:** Enhancing the
brightness and glow of bright areas in the scene, simulating the
effect of intense light sources. 3. **Depth of Field:** Simulating the
way a camera focuses on objects, blurring objects that are out of
focus. 4. **Motion Blur:** Blurring objects in motion to create a
sense of speed and realism. 5. **Lens Flares:** Simulating the
scattering of light in the camera lens, creating characteristic
artifacts. 6. **HDR Tone Mapping:** Mapping high dynamic range
(HDR) images to the limited dynamic range of standard displays.
7. **Anti-Aliasing:** Reducing jagged edges and improving the
overall smoothness of rendered images. ### Implementing Post-
Processing Effects in Vulkan

To implement post-processing effects in Vulkan, you can follow
these general steps: 1. **Framebuffer Setup:** Create one or more
framebuffers to store intermediate images during the post-
processing pipeline. These framebuffers act as textures that can
be used as inputs and outputs for each post-processing pass. 2.
**Shader Programs:** Develop shader programs that define the
specific post-processing effect you want to achieve. These
shaders operate on the intermediate images or the final image. 3.
**Rendering Passes:** Create a series of rendering passes, where
each pass uses a shader to perform a specific post-processing
operation. These passes can be chained together, with the output
of one pass becoming the input to the next. 4. **Image Blitting:** If
necessary, you may need to perform image blitting or copying
operations between framebuffers to transition data between
passes. 5. **Final Composite:** After applying all desired post-
processing passes, the final composited image is available in a
framebuffer. This image can be presented to the screen or
further processed as needed. ### Challenges and Considerations

Implementing post-processing effects in Vulkan comes with challenges related to performance, memory management, and synchronization between rendering passes. Some effects, like motion blur, may require additional data or information from previous frames.

Optimizations, such as downsampling the image for certain passes and using mipmaps, can help improve performance. Additionally, it's essential to handle resource management efficiently to avoid memory leaks and fragmentation.

The choice of which post-processing effects to implement depends on the specific requirements of your application and the visual style you aim to achieve. Experimentation and fine-tuning are often necessary to achieve the desired results.

In summary, post-processing effects are a valuable tool in Vulkan for enhancing the visual quality and realism of rendered scenes. By carefully designing shaders and rendering passes, you can achieve impressive and visually appealing effects in your Vulkan applications, adding depth and immersion to your graphics.

# Chapter 8: Optimizing Graphics Performance

## Section 8.1: Profiling and Performance Analysis

Optimizing graphics performance is a critical aspect of graphics programming, as it directly impacts the quality and smoothness of the user experience. Profiling and performance analysis are essential techniques for identifying bottlenecks, optimizing code, and ensuring that your application runs efficiently. In this section, we'll delve into the importance of profiling and performance analysis in Vulkan applications and explore how to use various tools and techniques to improve performance. ### The Significance of Profiling

Profiling involves measuring the execution time and resource usage of different parts of your application to identify performance bottlenecks. In Vulkan programming, it helps you pinpoint areas where rendering, computation, or memory operations are taking more time than expected. Profiling provides valuable insights into how your application utilizes the CPU and GPU resources, helping you identify areas for improvement.

Profiling is crucial for the following reasons: 1. **Identifying Performance Bottlenecks:** Profiling helps you discover which parts of your code or rendering pipeline are causing performance issues. It could be due to inefficient algorithms, resource overutilization, or poor CPU-GPU synchronization. 2. **Optimization Targeting:** Once you identify bottlenecks, you can focus your optimization efforts on the specific areas that need improvement, saving time and effort. 3. **Resource Management:** Profiling helps you manage GPU and CPU resources efficiently. You can monitor memory usage, detect memory leaks, and ensure that resources are released when no longer needed. ### Profiling Tools and Techniques

To perform effective profiling in Vulkan applications, you can use various tools and techniques: 1. **Vulkan Validation Layers:** Vulkan provides validation layers that can detect errors, warnings, and performance issues during development. These layers can be instrumental in identifying Vulkan-related problems early in the development process. 2. **GPU Profiling Tools:** Modern GPUs come with profiling tools provided by GPU manufacturers (e.g., NVIDIA Nsight, AMD Radeon GPU Profiler). These tools allow you to capture and analyze GPU performance metrics, such as GPU utilization, memory usage, and shader performance. 3. **CPU Profiling Tools:** Profilers like Intel VTune, AMD CodeXL, and various open-source CPU profilers help you analyze CPU performance. They can identify CPU bottlenecks, thread synchronization issues, and hotspots in your code. 4. **Frame Timing Analysis:** Measuring frame times and frame rates is essential for assessing the overall performance of your application. Tools like RenderDoc and the built-in Vulkan timestamp queries can help you analyze frame timing and identify frame spikes. 5. **Memory Profiling:** Memory profiling tools can help you track memory allocations, detect memory leaks, and ensure efficient memory management. 6. **Custom Profiling Code:** You can also instrument your code with custom profiling markers to measure the execution time of specific functions or code blocks. Vulkan provides mechanisms for this purpose. ### Profiling Best Practices

When conducting profiling and performance analysis in Vulkan, consider the following best practices: - **Profiling in Realistic Scenarios:** Profile your application under realistic conditions and scenarios to ensure that the measurements accurately reflect the user experience. - **Regular Profiling Iterations:** Profiling should be an iterative process throughout the development cycle. Regularly profile your application, identify bottlenecks, make optimizations, and profile again to gauge the impact of your changes. - **Optimization Trade-offs:** Be mindful of optimization trade-offs. Some optimizations may improve one aspect of performance but adversely affect another. Consider the overall impact on the user experience. - **Cross-Platform Profiling:** If you're targeting multiple platforms (e.g., Windows, Linux, macOS), profile on each platform to address platform-specific performance issues. - **Documentation and Analysis:** Maintain documentation of profiling results, optimizations made, and their impact. Analyze trends over time to identify long-term performance improvements.

In conclusion, profiling and performance analysis are essential tools for optimizing graphics performance in Vulkan applications. By using profiling tools and techniques, you can pinpoint performance bottlenecks, make targeted optimizations, and ensure that your application delivers a smooth and responsive user experience. Profiling should be an integral part of your graphics programming workflow to achieve optimal performance.

## Section 8.2: Vulkan Validation Layers

Vulkan validation layers are a set of runtime checks and debugging tools provided by the Vulkan SDK to help developers identify and fix issues in their Vulkan applications. These layers are particularly useful during development and debugging phases, as they can catch common mistakes, ensure proper API usage, and provide detailed error messages. In this section, we'll explore Vulkan validation layers, their significance, and how to use them effectively in your graphics programming projects.

### Importance of Vulkan Validation Layers

Vulkan is designed to be a low-level and explicit graphics API, which gives developers a high degree of control over the hardware. However, this control comes with the responsibility of correctly managing resources, synchronization, and other aspects of GPU programming. Mistakes in Vulkan can lead to crashes, rendering artifacts, and hard-to-debug issues.

Validation layers play a crucial role in the Vulkan development workflow for several reasons: 1. **Error Detection:** Validation layers can detect common programming errors, such as incorrect API usage, invalid parameters, and memory leaks, before they lead to more significant issues. 2. **Debugging Aid:** When an error is detected, validation layers provide detailed error messages, making it easier to pinpoint the exact problem in your code. 3. **Cross-Platform Consistency:** Vulkan validation layers help ensure that your code behaves consistently across different platforms and GPU vendors. They enforce Vulkan specification rules, helping you avoid vendor-specific behaviors. 4. **Performance Insights:** Validation layers can also provide performance-related warnings and recommendations, helping you identify potential bottlenecks and areas for optimization.

### Enabling Vulkan Validation Layers

To use Vulkan validation layers effectively, follow these steps: 1. **Enable Validation Layers during Instance Creation:** When creating a Vulkan instance, specify the validation layers you want to enable in the VkInstanceCreateInfo structure. You can specify the layers using the ppEnabledLayerNames field.

```
VkInstanceCreateInfo createInfo = {};
createInfo.sType =
VK_STRUCTURE_TYPE_INSTANCE_CREATE_INFO;
```

```
// Enable validation Layers
const char* validationLayers[] = {
"VK_LAYER_KHRONOS_validation" };
createInfo.ppEnabledLayerNames = validationLayers;
createInfo.enabledLayerCount = sizeof(validationLayers)
/ sizeof(validationLayers[0]);

// ...
```

2. **Set Up Debug Callback:** To receive validation layer
   messages and errors, you can set up a debug callback
   function using the
   VkDebugUtilsMessengerCreateInfoEXT structure. This
   allows you to specify how validation layer messages
   should be handled.

```
VkDebugUtilsMessengerCreateInfoEXT debugCreateInfo =
{};
debugCreateInfo.sType =
VK_STRUCTURE_TYPE_DEBUG_UTILS_MESSENGER_CREATE_INFO_EXT
;
debugCreateInfo.messageSeverity =
VK_DEBUG_UTILS_MESSAGE_SEVERITY_WARNING_BIT_EXT |

VK_DEBUG_UTILS_MESSAGE_SEVERITY_ERROR_BIT_EXT;
debugCreateInfo.messageType =
VK_DEBUG_UTILS_MESSAGE_TYPE_GENERAL_BIT_EXT |

VK_DEBUG_UTILS_MESSAGE_TYPE_VALIDATION_BIT_EXT;
debugCreateInfo.pfnUserCallback = debugCallback;
debugCreateInfo.pUserData = nullptr;
```

3. **Register the Debug Callback:** Register the debug
   callback function with Vulkan using the
   vkCreateDebugUtilsMessengerEXT function.

```
VkDebugUtilsMessengerEXT debugMessenger;
if (CreateDebugUtilsMessengerEXT(instance,
&debugCreateInfo, nullptr, &debugMessenger) !=
VK_SUCCESS) {
    // Handle error
}
```

4.  **Handle Validation Messages:** In the debug callback
    function (debugCallback in the example above), you can
    handle validation layer messages as desired. You may
    choose to log them, display them in the application, or
    take specific actions based on the severity and type of
    message.

```
VKAPI_ATTR VkBool32 VKAPI_CALL debugCallback(
    VkDebugUtilsMessageSeverityFlagBitsEXT
messageSeverity,
    VkDebugUtilsMessageTypeFlagsEXT messageType,
    const VkDebugUtilsMessengerCallbackDataEXT*
pCallbackData,
    void* pUserData) {

    // Handle validation message based on severity and
type

    return VK_FALSE; // Return VK_TRUE to abort the
Vulkan call that triggered this callback
}
```

### Validation Layer Tips and Considerations

When using Vulkan validation layers, keep the following tips and
considerations in mind: - **Performance Impact:** Enabling
validation layers can impact application performance, especially
in release builds. Therefore, it's common to disable validation
layers in production builds for better performance. - **Custom
Validation Layers:** You can create custom validation layers
tailored to your application's specific requirements. This can be
helpful for enforcing project-specific coding standards and
practices. - **Validation Layer Extension:** Vulkan validation
layers are implemented as an extension, so you need to query
and load the extension functions if you want to use them.
Additionally, different Vulkan SDKs may have variations in
available validation layers. - **Update Validation Layer
Information:** Keep your Vulkan SDK and validation layers up to
date to benefit from the latest bug fixes and improvements.

In conclusion, Vulkan validation layers are indispensable tools for debugging and ensuring the correctness of Vulkan applications. They help catch errors and provide valuable insights into Vulkan API usage, improving the development and maintenance of graphics applications. However, it's essential to use validation layers judiciously and consider their performance impact when developing Vulkan projects.

## Section 8.3: Pipeline Caching and Reuse

Pipeline caching is a crucial optimization technique in Vulkan graphics programming. It involves the creation and reuse of graphics pipelines, which are a combination of shaders, configuration settings, and state objects that define how rendering operations are executed. By effectively managing pipelines, you can reduce the overhead of pipeline creation and improve the overall performance of your Vulkan application. In this section, we'll delve into the importance of pipeline caching and how to implement it in your graphics programming projects. ### The Significance of Pipeline Caching

In Vulkan, creating graphics pipelines is a complex and resource-intensive operation. Each pipeline creation involves parsing and compiling shaders, setting up pipeline configurations, and allocating memory. In dynamic scenes or applications with frequent pipeline changes, the overhead of pipeline creation can become a significant performance bottleneck.

Pipeline caching addresses this issue by allowing you to save and reuse pipelines. Once a pipeline is created and cached, you can reuse it for subsequent rendering operations that share the same configuration. This reduces the time and resources required for pipeline creation, resulting in smoother and more efficient rendering. ### Pipeline Cache Types

Vulkan provides two types of pipeline caches: 1. **Pipeline Cache Object (VkPipelineCache):** This is a Vulkan object that represents a pipeline cache. It can be created and managed by your application. 2. **Pipeline Cache File:** In addition to the pipeline cache object, Vulkan allows you to create a pipeline cache file that can be stored on disk. This file can be reused across application runs and even on different devices. ### Creating and Using Pipeline Caches

To implement pipeline caching in your Vulkan application, follow these steps: 1. **Create a Pipeline Cache Object:** Create a pipeline cache object using the vkCreatePipelineCache function. You can associate this object with your Vulkan device.

```
VkPipelineCacheCreateInfo cacheCreateInfo = {};
cacheCreateInfo.sType =
VK_STRUCTURE_TYPE_PIPELINE_CACHE_CREATE_INFO;

VkPipelineCache pipelineCache;
if (vkCreatePipelineCache(device, &cacheCreateInfo,
nullptr, &pipelineCache) != VK_SUCCESS) {
    // Handle error
}
```

2. **Serialize and Deserialize Pipeline Cache Data:** To save and load pipeline cache data from a file, you can use the vkGetPipelineCacheData and vkMergePipelineCaches functions. Serialization allows you to save pipeline cache data to a file, and deserialization enables you to reuse that data in subsequent runs.

```
size_t dataSize;
if (vkGetPipelineCacheData(device, pipelineCache,
&dataSize, nullptr) != VK_SUCCESS) {
    // Handle error
}

std::vector<uint8_t> cacheData(dataSize);
if (vkGetPipelineCacheData(device, pipelineCache,
&dataSize, cacheData.data()) != VK_SUCCESS) {
    // Handle error
}

// Save cacheData to a file for later use
```

```
// When initializing a new pipeline cache, you can
merge cached data from a file:
VkPipelineCache newPipelineCache;
VkPipelineCache oldPipelineCaches[] = {
pipelineCacheFromFile1, pipelineCacheFromFile2 };
if (vkCreatePipelineCache(device, &cacheCreateInfo,
nullptr, &newPipelineCache) != VK_SUCCESS) {
    // Handle error
}
vkMergePipelineCaches(device, newPipelineCache,
sizeof(oldPipelineCaches) /
sizeof(oldPipelineCaches[0]), oldPipelineCaches);
```

3. **Use the Pipeline Cache in Pipeline Creation:** When
   creating a graphics pipeline, you can pass the pipeline
   cache object to the VkGraphicsPipelineCreateInfo
   structure to specify that the pipeline should be created
   from the cached data.

```
VkGraphicsPipelineCreateInfo pipelineInfo = {};
pipelineInfo.sType =
VK_STRUCTURE_TYPE_GRAPHICS_PIPELINE_CREATE_INFO;
pipelineInfo.pCacheData = cacheData.data(); // Specify
the cache data
// Other pipeline creation parameters...
```

By following these steps, you can effectively manage and reuse
graphics pipelines in your Vulkan application, reducing the
overhead of pipeline creation and improving overall rendering
performance. Pipeline caching is especially beneficial in
scenarios where pipelines are frequently created and used, such
as dynamic scenes or applications with a wide range of
rendering configurations.

## Section 8.4: Efficient Rendering Techniques

Efficient rendering is a critical aspect of graphics programming,
especially when working with real-time applications and
complex scenes. In this section, we will explore various
techniques and strategies for optimizing rendering performance
in Vulkan. ### 1. **Batch Rendering:**

One of the fundamental techniques for efficient rendering is batch rendering. It involves grouping similar objects or primitives together and rendering them in a single draw call. This reduces the overhead associated with multiple draw calls and state changes. Vulkan provides support for instanced rendering and indirect drawing, which can be employed for efficient batch rendering.

```
// Example of instanced rendering
vkCmdDrawIndexed(cmdBuffer, indexCount, instanceCount,
firstIndex, 0, 0);


// Example of indirect drawing
vkCmdDrawIndexedIndirect(cmdBuffer, buffer, offset,
drawCount, stride);
```

**Dynamic Uniform Buffers:**

Vulkan allows for dynamic uniform buffers, where frequently changing data can be updated in a buffer and bound to shaders without recreating pipelines. This is particularly useful for objects with varying transformations, such as animated characters.

```
// Update uniform buffer data
void* data;
vkMapMemory(device, uniformBufferMemory, 0,
sizeof(UniformBufferObject), 0, &data);
memcpy(data, &ubo, sizeof(UniformBufferObject));
vkUnmapMemory(device, uniformBufferMemory);


// Bind the updated uniform buffer
VkDescriptorBufferInfo bufferInfo = {};
bufferInfo.buffer = uniformBuffer;
bufferInfo.offset = 0;
bufferInfo.range = sizeof(UniformBufferObject);
```

**Level of Detail (LOD):**

LOD techniques involve rendering objects at different levels of detail based on their distance from the viewer. Vulkan supports

LOD bias, which allows you to adjust the level of detail for textures and models dynamically.

```
// Set LOD bias for a texture
VkSamplerCreateInfo samplerInfo = {};
samplerInfo.mipmapMode = VK_SAMPLER_MIPMAP_MODE_LINEAR;
samplerInfo.mipLodBias = lodBias;
```

**Occlusion Culling:**

Occlusion culling is a technique used to avoid rendering objects that are not visible to the camera. Vulkan provides support for occlusion queries, which can be used to determine if an object is occluded by others before rendering it.

```
// Begin occlusion query
vkCmdBeginQuery(cmdBuffer, queryPool, queryIndex,
VK_QUERY_CONTROL_PRECISE_BIT);

// Render objects

// End occlusion query
vkCmdEndQuery(cmdBuffer, queryPool, queryIndex);
```

**Multithreading:**

Leveraging multithreading can significantly improve rendering performance by parallelizing tasks like command buffer recording and data uploading. Vulkan's explicit control over threading makes it well-suited for multi-core processors.

```
// Create multiple threads for rendering tasks
std::thread thread1(RenderThreadFunction);
std::thread thread2(RenderThreadFunction);
// ...

// Wait for threads to finish
thread1.join();
thread2.join();
```

**Resource Reuse and Management:**

Efficient resource management involves reusing memory and objects wherever possible. Vulkan's memory management and object reuse capabilities allow you to allocate and recycle resources effectively.

```
// Reuse memory and resources when creating new objects
```

These are just a few of the many techniques available for optimizing rendering performance in Vulkan. The specific strategies you choose will depend on the requirements of your application and the complexity of your scenes. Profiling and benchmarking your application is crucial to identifying bottlenecks and determining which optimizations will have the most significant impact on performance.

## Section 8.5: GPU and CPU Synchronization

Efficient synchronization between the GPU (Graphics Processing Unit) and CPU (Central Processing Unit) is vital for maintaining smooth and correct rendering in Vulkan. In this section, we'll explore the various synchronization mechanisms and best practices for managing interactions between the CPU and GPU in your Vulkan applications. ### 1. **Semaphores:**

Semaphores are synchronization objects used to coordinate GPU and CPU operations. They ensure that certain GPU operations are complete before CPU operations proceed and vice versa. You can use semaphores to synchronize image acquisition, rendering, and presentation.

```
// Example of semaphore usage for synchronization
VkSemaphore imageAvailableSemaphore;
VkSemaphore renderFinishedSemaphore;

// CPU-GPU synchronization
VkSemaphoreCreateInfo semaphoreInfo = {};
semaphoreInfo.sType =
VK_STRUCTURE_TYPE_SEMAPHORE_CREATE_INFO;
```

```cpp
vkCreateSemaphore(device, &semaphoreInfo, nullptr,
&imageAvailableSemaphore);
vkCreateSemaphore(device, &semaphoreInfo, nullptr,
&renderFinishedSemaphore);
```

Fences:

Fences are synchronization primitives that allow you to wait for GPU operations to complete from the CPU. They are useful for CPU-GPU synchronization and ensuring that GPU work has finished before proceeding.

```cpp
// Example of fence usage for CPU-GPU synchronization
VkFence fence;

VkFenceCreateInfo fenceInfo = {};
fenceInfo.sType = VK_STRUCTURE_TYPE_FENCE_CREATE_INFO;
fenceInfo.flags = VK_FENCE_CREATE_SIGNALED_BIT; //
Create the fence in a signaled state

vkCreateFence(device, &fenceInfo, nullptr, &fence);

// Wait for the fence to become signaled (GPU work
complete)
vkWaitForFences(device, 1, &fence, VK_TRUE,
UINT64_MAX);
```

Pipeline Barriers:

Pipeline barriers are used to synchronize memory access between different pipeline stages in Vulkan. They allow you to control the order and timing of memory reads and writes, ensuring data integrity and correctness.

```cpp
// Example of pipeline barrier usage
VkPipelineStageFlags sourceStage =
VK_PIPELINE_STAGE_TRANSFER_BIT;
VkPipelineStageFlags destinationStage =
VK_PIPELINE_STAGE_FRAGMENT_SHADER_BIT;

VkImageMemoryBarrier barrier = {};
barrier.sType = VK_STRUCTURE_TYPE_IMAGE_MEMORY_BARRIER;
```

```
barrier.oldLayout = VK_IMAGE_LAYOUT_UNDEFINED;
barrier.newLayout =
VK_IMAGE_LAYOUT_TRANSFER_DST_OPTIMAL;
barrier.srcQueueFamilyIndex = VK_QUEUE_FAMILY_IGNORED;
barrier.dstQueueFamilyIndex = VK_QUEUE_FAMILY_IGNORED;
barrier.image = image;
barrier.subresourceRange = { VK_IMAGE_ASPECT_COLOR_BIT,
0, 1, 0, 1 };

vkCmdPipelineBarrier(commandBuffer, sourceStage,
destinationStage, 0, 0, nullptr, 0, nullptr, 1,
&barrier);
```

**Resource Ownership and Lifetimes:**

Vulkan requires careful management of resource ownership and lifetimes. Resources like command buffers, images, and memory must be allocated and deallocated appropriately to avoid resource leaks.

```
// Allocate and free resources
vkAllocateCommandBuffers(device, &cmdBufferInfo,
&commandBuffer);
vkFreeCommandBuffers(device, commandPool, 1,
&commandBuffer);
```

**Render Passes and Subpasses:**

Vulkan's render pass and subpass system provides explicit control over synchronization between rendering operations. By specifying dependencies between subpasses, you can ensure correct ordering and synchronization of GPU work.

```
// Example of subpass dependency declaration
VkSubpassDependency dependency = {};
dependency.srcSubpass = VK_SUBPASS_EXTERNAL;
dependency.dstSubpass = 0;
dependency.srcStageMask =
VK_PIPELINE_STAGE_COLOR_ATTACHMENT_OUTPUT_BIT;
dependency.srcAccessMask = 0;
dependency.dstStageMask =
VK_PIPELINE_STAGE_COLOR_ATTACHMENT_OUTPUT_BIT;
```

```
dependency.dstAccessMask =
VK_ACCESS_COLOR_ATTACHMENT_WRITE_BIT;
```

**Command Buffer Submission:**

Proper submission of command buffers to queues is essential for
CPU-GPU synchronization. You must ensure that command
buffers are submitted in the correct order and that their
execution is synchronized as needed.

```
// Submit command buffer to a queue
VkSubmitInfo submitInfo = {};
submitInfo.sType = VK_STRUCTURE_TYPE_SUBMIT_INFO;
submitInfo.commandBufferCount = 1;
submitInfo.pCommandBuffers = &commandBuffer;

vkQueueSubmit(queue, 1, &submitInfo, VK_NULL_HANDLE);
```

Synchronization in Vulkan can be complex due to its explicit
nature, but it provides fine-grained control over GPU-CPU
interactions. Properly managing synchronization is crucial for
achieving both correctness and optimal performance in your
graphics applications. Careful consideration of semaphores,
fences, pipeline barriers, resource lifetimes, render passes, and
command buffer submission is necessary to ensure smooth and
efficient operation in Vulkan.

# Chapter 9: Cross-Platform Development

## Section 9.1: Introduction to Cross-Platform Development

Cross-platform development is a crucial aspect of graphics
programming. It involves creating applications that can run on
multiple operating systems (OS) or platforms without significant
modification. This approach ensures wider reach and
accessibility for your graphics software. In this section, we'll
delve into the fundamentals of cross-platform development, the
challenges it presents, and the strategies to address them. ### 1.
**Why Cross-Platform Development?**

Developing software for a single platform limits its user base and may not be feasible for certain projects. Cross-platform development allows you to reach users on various platforms, including Windows, Linux, macOS, and even mobile devices. It can reduce development costs and effort in the long run. ### 2. **Challenges in Cross-Platform Development:**

Cross-platform development comes with its own set of challenges, such as: - **Diverse APIs:** Each platform may have its own set of graphics APIs (e.g., DirectX on Windows, Metal on macOS, and Vulkan on various platforms). Handling these differences requires careful planning. - **User Interface:** Different platforms have distinct user interface guidelines and paradigms. Adapting your application's UI to each platform can be complex. - **Performance Variations:** Hardware capabilities and performance characteristics vary between platforms. Optimizing for different hardware is essential. - **Input Handling:** Handling input from different devices and platforms (e.g., touch input on mobile vs. keyboard and mouse on desktop) can be challenging. ### 3. **Cross-Platform Development Approaches:**

Several approaches can be adopted for cross-platform development: - **Platform Abstraction Libraries:** Use libraries like SDL (Simple DirectMedia Layer), GLFW, or Qt that provide a unified interface for graphics, input, and window management across platforms. - **Web Technologies:** Develop applications using web technologies like HTML5, CSS, and JavaScript, then package them as native apps using frameworks like Electron or React Native. - **Game Engines:** Game engines like Unity or Unreal Engine offer cross-platform support for graphics and game development. - **Native Development:** Write platform-specific code for each OS, but share common core logic and resources. This approach requires more effort but provides fine-grained control. ### 4. **Choosing the Right Approach:**

The choice of approach depends on factors like your project's complexity, target audience, and available resources. Consider the following when making a decision: - **Project Scope:** Simple applications may benefit from platform abstraction libraries, while complex games might require a game engine. - **Performance Requirements:** For high-performance graphics applications, native development may be preferred to have more control over optimization. - **Development Team:** Consider the skills and expertise of your development team in different technologies. - **Budget and Time:** Assess your project's budget and timeline, as certain approaches may require more time and resources. ### 5. **Development Workflow:**

Cross-platform development often involves maintaining multiple codebases for different platforms. A version control system (e.g., Git) can help manage code synchronization and collaboration among team members.

Continuous integration (CI) and automated testing are crucial to ensure that changes made on one platform do not break functionality on others. ### 6. **Testing and Debugging:**

Rigorous testing on all target platforms is essential. Emulators, simulators, and physical devices can help simulate different environments.

Debugging tools provided by platform-specific SDKs and IDEs should be utilized for efficient bug tracking and resolution.

Cross-platform development opens up opportunities to reach a broader audience with your graphics applications. By understanding the challenges, choosing the right approach, and maintaining a robust development workflow, you can successfully create graphics software that runs seamlessly on various operating systems and devices.

## Section 9.2: Using Platform Abstraction Libraries

Platform abstraction libraries are valuable tools in the toolkit of a cross-platform graphics developer. These libraries provide a unified interface for handling graphics, window management, input, and more across multiple platforms. They abstract away the platform-specific details, allowing you to write code that works consistently across different operating systems. In this section, we'll explore the use of platform abstraction libraries and how they simplify cross-platform graphics programming.

### 1. **Popular Platform Abstraction Libraries:**

There are several platform abstraction libraries available, each with its own strengths and areas of focus. Some of the most popular ones include: - **SDL (Simple DirectMedia Layer):** SDL is a widely used library that provides simple and efficient access to graphics, audio, input, and more. It supports Windows, macOS, Linux, iOS, Android, and more. - **GLFW:** GLFW is a lightweight library specifically designed for creating and managing windows with OpenGL contexts. It is known for its simplicity and cross-platform support, covering Windows, macOS, and Linux. - **SFML (Simple and Fast Multimedia Library):** SFML is a multimedia library that offers features for graphics, audio, and network communication. It is portable and supports multiple platforms, including Windows, macOS, and Linux. - **Qt:** Qt is a comprehensive framework for building cross-platform applications with a strong emphasis on GUI development. It supports Windows, macOS, Linux, and mobile platforms. - **FreeGLUT:** FreeGLUT is an open-source alternative to the OpenGL Utility Toolkit (GLUT) library, providing window and input management. It is portable across various platforms. ### 2. **Advantages of Using Platform Abstraction Libraries:** - **Simplified Development:** These libraries abstract away the complexities of platform-specific APIs, making it easier to focus on the core logic of your graphics application. - **Cross-Platform Compatibility:** Code written using these libraries can be compiled and run on different platforms with minimal or no modifications. - **Consistent User Experience:** By using a unified interface for window creation, input handling, and other tasks, you can ensure a consistent user experience across platforms. - **Community and Documentation:** Popular libraries like SDL and GLFW have active communities and extensive documentation, making it easier to find help and resources. ### 3. **Basic Usage:**

Here's a simplified example using GLFW to create a window and set up an OpenGL context:

```c
#include <GLFW/glfw3.h>

int main() {
    // Initialize GLFW
    if (!glfwInit()) {
        return -1;
    }

    // Create a windowed mode window and its OpenGL
context
    GLFWwindow* window = glfwCreateWindow(640, 480, "My
OpenGL Window", NULL, NULL);
    if (!window) {
        glfwTerminate();
        return -1;
    }

    // Make the window's context current
    glfwMakeContextCurrent(window);

    // Main Loop
    while (!glfwWindowShouldClose(window)) {
        // Render here

        // Swap front and back buffers
        glfwSwapBuffers(window);

        // Poll for and process events
        glfwPollEvents();
    }

    // Terminate GLFW
    glfwTerminate();
    return 0;
}
```

This code initializes GLFW, creates a window, sets up an OpenGL context, and enters a loop for rendering and event handling. ###
4. **Limitations and Considerations:**

While platform abstraction libraries offer many benefits, there are some considerations to keep in mind: - **Limited Control:** Abstraction libraries may limit your control over certain platform-specific features. If your application requires fine-grained control, you may need to use platform-specific code in addition to the library. - **Performance Overheads:** Abstraction layers can introduce some performance overhead compared to direct platform-specific code. However, for most applications, this overhead is negligible. - **Platform-Specific Features:** Some advanced platform-specific features may not be accessible through abstraction libraries. In such cases, you may need to resort to platform-specific code or extensions.

Platform abstraction libraries are excellent tools for simplifying cross-platform graphics development. They save time, ensure consistency, and allow developers to focus on their application's core logic. When choosing a library, consider your specific requirements and the platforms you intend to target to make the best choice for your project.

## Section 9.3: Building for Windows, Linux, and macOS

Building cross-platform graphics applications often involves compiling and packaging your code for different operating systems. In this section, we will explore the process of building and distributing your graphics application on three popular desktop platforms: Windows, Linux, and macOS. Each platform has its own set of tools and conventions for building and distributing software. ### 1. **Building for Windows:** #### Development Environment: - On Windows, Visual Studio is a popular integrated development environment (IDE) for C/C++ programming. You can use Visual Studio's project templates to create Windows applications. #### Compilation: - Visual Studio provides a straightforward build process. You typically create a project, add your source files, configure build settings, and then build the application. #### Packaging: - Windows applications are often distributed as .exe files. You can use tools like Inno Setup or NSIS (Nullsoft Scriptable Install System) to create installers for your application. ### 2. **Building for Linux:** ####

Development Environment: - Linux provides a range of development tools, including GCC (GNU Compiler Collection) for C/C++ development. You can use text editors like Visual Studio Code or IDEs like Qt Creator. #### Compilation: - Compiling on Linux usually involves using the terminal and a Makefile or build script. You can use GCC to compile your code into an executable binary. #### Packaging: - Linux distributions use package managers like APT (Debian/Ubuntu) or RPM (Red Hat/Fedora). You can create packages (e.g., .deb or .rpm) for your application to simplify installation. ### 3. **Building for macOS:** #### Development Environment: - On macOS, Xcode is the primary IDE for C/C++ development. You can create macOS applications using Xcode projects. #### Compilation: - Xcode provides a user-friendly interface for building applications. You configure build settings, add source files, and then build your project. #### Packaging: - macOS applications are typically distributed as .app bundles. You can use Xcode to create a .app bundle, which includes your executable, resources, and icons. ### 4. **Cross-Platform Considerations:** #### Using Cross-Platform Libraries: - To simplify cross-platform development, consider using platform abstraction libraries like GLFW or SDL, as discussed in Section 9.2. These libraries can help ensure consistent behavior across different operating systems. #### Conditional Compilation: - You may need to use conditional compilation directives (#ifdef, #ifndef, etc.) to include or exclude platform-specific code in your source files.

```
#ifdef _WIN32
    // Windows-specific code
#elif __linux__
    // Linux-specific code
#elif __APPLE__
    // macOS-specific code
#endif
```

Continuous Integration:

- Setting up a continuous integration (CI) system can be beneficial for automatically building and testing your application on multiple platforms. Services like Jenkins,

Travis CI, or GitHub Actions can help streamline this process. ### 6. **User Experience:**

- Keep in mind that each platform has its own user interface guidelines and conventions. To provide the best user experience, adapt your application's UI to the platform it's running on.

Building cross-platform graphics applications requires careful consideration of the development environment, compilation process, and packaging methods for each target platform. While it may require some extra effort, the ability to reach a wider audience and provide a consistent experience on different operating systems can be well worth it for your graphics project.

## Section 9.4: Handling Input and Windowing

In the context of graphics programming, handling input and windowing are crucial aspects of creating interactive applications. Users need a way to interact with your graphics application, and the application needs a window or viewport to display graphics output. In this section, we will explore how to manage input from various devices and create windows for your graphics applications on different platforms. ### 1. **Input Handling:** #### Keyboard Input: - To handle keyboard input, you typically need to capture keypresses and key releases. You can use platform-specific APIs or cross-platform libraries like GLFW or SDL to handle keyboard events. - Here's a simplified example using GLFW in C++ to capture keyboard input:

```cpp
#include <GLFW/glfw3.h>

void key_callback(GLFWwindow* window, int key, int scancode, int action, int mods) {
    if (action == GLFW_PRESS) {
        // Key was pressed
        if (key == GLFW_KEY_ESCAPE) {
            // Handle the ESC key press
        }
    }
}
```

```cpp
int main() {
    // Initialize GLFW and create a window
    // ...

    // Set the key callback function
    glfwSetKeyCallback(window, key_callback);

    // Main loop
    while (!glfwWindowShouldClose(window)) {
        // Render graphics
        // ...

        // Poll for events (including key events)
        glfwPollEvents();
    }

    // Cleanup and exit
    // ...

    return 0;
}
```

*Mouse Input:*

- Handling mouse input involves tracking mouse movements and clicks. You can use similar libraries like GLFW or SDL to manage mouse events.
- Here's a simplified example using GLFW in C++ to capture mouse input:

```cpp
void mouse_button_callback(GLFWwindow* window, int button, int action, int mods) {
    if (action == GLFW_PRESS) {
        // Mouse button was pressed
        if (button == GLFW_MOUSE_BUTTON_LEFT) {
            // Handle left mouse button click
        }
    }
}

void cursor_position_callback(GLFWwindow* window,
```

```cpp
double xpos, double ypos) {
    // Track cursor position
    // ...
}

int main() {
    // Initialize GLFW and create a window
    // ...

    // Set mouse button callback function
    glfwSetMouseButtonCallback(window,
mouse_button_callback);

    // Set cursor position callback function
    glfwSetCursorPosCallback(window,
cursor_position_callback);

    // Main loop
    // ...

    return 0;
}
```

*Gamepad and Controller Input:*

- For gamepad and controller input, you can use platform-specific APIs or libraries like SDL or gamepad-specific libraries (e.g., XInput on Windows) to handle input from game controllers. ### 2. **Windowing:** #### Creating a Window:

- To create a window for your graphics application, you can use platform-specific APIs or cross-platform libraries like GLFW or SDL.

- Here's a simplified example using GLFW in C++ to create a window:

```cpp
#include <GLFW/glfw3.h>

int main() {
    // Initialize GLFW
    if (!glfwInit()) {
```

```
        // Initialization failed
        return -1;
    }

    // Create a windowed mode window
    GLFWwindow* window = glfwCreateWindow(800, 600, "My
Graphics App", NULL, NULL);
    if (!window) {
        // Window creation failed
        glfwTerminate();
        return -1;
    }

    // Make the window's context current
    glfwMakeContextCurrent(window);

    // Main loop
    while (!glfwWindowShouldClose(window)) {
        // Render graphics
        // ...

        // Swap front and back buffers
        glfwSwapBuffers(window);

        // Poll for events (including window events)
        glfwPollEvents();
    }

    // Cleanup and exit
    glfwTerminate();
    return 0;
}
```

*Window Resizing:*

- You may need to handle window resizing events to adapt
  your graphics output to the new window size. GLFW and
  other libraries provide mechanisms to detect and
  respond to window size changes.

Managing input and windowing is essential for creating
interactive graphics applications. Depending on your target

platform and requirements, you can choose the appropriate libraries and techniques for input handling and window creation. These examples provide a starting point, but more complex applications may require additional input and window management features.

## Section 9.5: Debugging and Testing on Multiple Platforms

Debugging and testing are critical aspects of graphics programming, ensuring that your application works correctly and efficiently across different platforms and configurations. In this section, we will explore strategies and tools for debugging and testing graphics applications on various platforms. ### 1. **Platform-Specific Debugging:**

Graphics programming often involves platform-specific code due to variations in APIs and drivers across different operating systems and hardware configurations. Here are some platform-specific debugging considerations: #### Windows Debugging: - For Windows development, Visual Studio provides robust debugging tools. You can set breakpoints, inspect variables, and use the Graphics Debugger to analyze GPU-related issues. - DirectX Graphics Debugging is available for debugging DirectX applications. It allows you to capture frames, examine GPU events, and identify rendering problems. - Tools like PIX (Performance Investigator for Xbox) can help debug graphics issues on Xbox platforms. #### macOS Debugging: - Xcode offers debugging tools for macOS and iOS development. It includes LLDB, a powerful debugger, and Instruments, a profiling and performance analysis tool. - Metal Shading Language Debugger (MSLDebugger) helps debug Metal-based graphics applications by allowing you to step through Metal shader code. #### Linux Debugging: - GDB (GNU Debugger) is a common choice for debugging on Linux. It supports debugging C/C++ code and can be used for graphics application debugging. - Vulkan validation layers can help identify errors in Vulkan applications on Linux. ### 2. **Cross-Platform Testing:**

To ensure your graphics application works consistently across platforms, you should perform cross-platform testing. Here are some strategies: #### Testing on Different Hardware: - Test your application on various hardware configurations to identify compatibility issues and performance variations. Consider using cloud-based testing services for broader coverage. #### Virtual Machines (VMs): - Use virtual machines to simulate different operating systems and configurations. Tools like VirtualBox, VMware, and Parallels Desktop allow you to run multiple virtual environments on a single physical machine. #### Emulators and Simulators: - When targeting mobile platforms, use emulators (Android) or simulators (iOS) to test on a range of devices and screen sizes without physical hardware. #### Continuous Integration (CI): - Implement a CI system to automate testing on multiple platforms. CI tools like Jenkins and Travis CI can build and test your graphics application on various platforms whenever changes are committed to the codebase. ### 3. **Performance Profiling:**

Performance profiling is crucial to identify bottlenecks and optimize your graphics application. Tools for profiling include: #### GPU Profilers: - NVIDIA Nsight and AMD Radeon GPU Profiler are tools for profiling GPU performance. They help analyze GPU usage, memory, and shader performance. #### CPU Profilers: - Profilers like Intel VTune and Linux perf can help identify CPU-related performance issues in graphics applications. #### Frame Capture: - Frame capture tools like RenderDoc and Apitrace allow you to capture frames and inspect graphics API calls. They are invaluable for diagnosing rendering problems. ### 4. **User Testing:**

Don't forget user testing, especially for applications with a user interface. Collect feedback from users on different platforms to identify usability issues and make necessary improvements. ### 5. **Documentation and Issue Tracking:**

Maintain thorough documentation of platform-specific issues and their solutions. Use issue tracking systems like JIRA or

GitHub Issues to manage and prioritize platform-related tasks.
### 6. **Version Control:**

Use version control systems like Git to manage your codebase. Create branches for platform-specific fixes and features to keep code organized and easily mergeable.

Debugging and testing on multiple platforms can be challenging, but it's essential to ensure a seamless user experience. By adopting the right tools and strategies, you can identify and resolve platform-specific issues, optimize performance, and deliver a reliable graphics application across a variety of platforms.

# Chapter 10: Best Practices and Tips

## Section 10.1: Coding Standards and Style Guidelines

Maintaining a consistent coding style and adhering to coding standards is crucial in graphics programming. It not only makes your codebase more readable but also helps in collaboration, debugging, and long-term maintenance. In this section, we'll discuss the importance of coding standards and provide some best practices and tips for creating clean and maintainable graphics code. ### 1. **Consistency in Naming Conventions:**

Choose a consistent naming convention for variables, functions, classes, and other identifiers. Common conventions include CamelCase, snake_case, and PascalCase. Stick to the convention used in your project or organization. ### 2. **Indentation and Formatting:**

Consistent indentation and code formatting are essential for readability. Use spaces or tabs consistently for indentation and establish rules for code layout. Code formatting tools like clang-format and Prettier can automate this process. ### 3. **Comments and Documentation:**

Document your code, especially complex algorithms and non-obvious decisions. Use meaningful comments to explain the purpose of functions, classes, and critical code sections. Consider generating API documentation using tools like Doxygen.

```
/**
 * @brief This function calculates the square of a
number.
 * @param x The input number.
 * @return The square of the input number.
 */
int CalculateSquare(int x) {
    return x * x;
}
```

Modularity and Abstraction:

Break your code into modular components and use abstraction to hide implementation details. This enhances code reusability and makes it easier to understand and maintain. ### 5. **Error Handling and Validation:**

Implement robust error handling mechanisms. Validate inputs and check for errors in graphics API calls. Proper error handling can prevent crashes and improve debugging.

```
// Vulkan API call with error checking
VkResult result = vkCreateDevice(device, &deviceInfo,
nullptr, &logicalDevice);
if (result != VK_SUCCESS) {
    // Handle error, log, or throw an exception.
}
```

Memory Management:

Graphics applications often deal with GPU memory. Proper memory management, including allocation and deallocation, is crucial to avoid memory leaks and performance issues. Use smart pointers and resource management libraries when applicable. ### 7. **Version Control:**

Use a version control system like Git to track changes, collaborate with others, and manage code versions. Follow best practices for branching, committing, and merging. ### 8. **Code Reviews:**

Conduct code reviews with team members to catch potential issues, enforce coding standards, and share knowledge. Code review tools like GitHub or GitLab can streamline this process. ### 9. **Testing and Continuous Integration:**

Implement automated testing and continuous integration (CI) to ensure code quality and prevent regressions. CI pipelines can run unit tests, static code analysis, and build checks on each code change. ### 10. **Static Code Analysis:**

Use static code analysis tools like Clang Static Analyzer, Coverity, or PVS-Studio to identify potential bugs, memory issues, and code smells in your graphics codebase. ### 11. **Coding Guidelines for Graphics APIs:**

Adhere to the coding guidelines and best practices specific to the graphics APIs you're using, such as OpenGL or Vulkan. API-specific guidelines often cover resource management, synchronization, and performance optimization. ### 12. **Performance Profiling:**

Regularly profile your graphics code to identify bottlenecks and areas for optimization. Profiling tools like GPU profilers, CPU profilers, and frame analyzers can help pinpoint performance issues. ### 13. **Code Refactoring:**

Periodically review and refactor your codebase to improve its design, performance, and maintainability. Refactoring should be driven by profiling data and code review feedback. ### 14. **Keep Learning:**

Graphics programming is a rapidly evolving field. Stay updated with the latest graphics APIs, techniques, and hardware advancements. Continuous learning is essential for writing efficient and cutting-edge graphics code.

In conclusion, following coding standards and style guidelines is essential for writing clean, maintainable, and reliable graphics code. Consistency in naming, proper documentation, modularity, and other best practices contribute to the overall quality of your graphics applications. Additionally, adopting tools and practices for error handling, testing, and profiling will help you create high-performance graphics software.

## Section 10.2: Version Control and Collaboration

Version control is an essential part of modern software development, including graphics programming. It enables multiple developers to collaborate on a codebase, track changes, and manage different versions of the code. In this section, we'll explore the importance of version control and effective collaboration strategies for graphics programming projects. ### Why Version Control Matters

Version control systems (VCS) like Git provide several benefits for graphics programming: 1. **History Tracking:** VCS records every change made to the codebase, including who made the change and when. This historical data is invaluable for debugging and understanding the evolution of the code. 2. **Collaboration:** Graphics projects often involve multiple team members. VCS allows developers to work simultaneously on different parts of the code and merge their changes seamlessly. 3. **Branching:** VCS enables the creation of branches, which are separate lines of development. Developers can work on new features or bug fixes in isolated branches without affecting the main codebase until changes are ready to be merged. 4. **Conflict Resolution:** When multiple developers modify the same code simultaneously, conflicts may arise. VCS provides tools to resolve conflicts and ensure code consistency. 5. **Code Reviews:** VCS platforms often integrate with code review tools, making it easy to conduct thorough code reviews. Code reviews enhance code quality and knowledge sharing. ### Choosing the Right VCS

While Git is the most popular VCS today, there are other options like Mercurial and Subversion. Graphics programming projects can benefit from Git due to its widespread adoption, robust branching model, and a wealth of available tools and hosting platforms (e.g., GitHub, GitLab, Bitbucket). ### Effective Collaboration Strategies

Here are some collaboration strategies to consider when using version control in graphics programming: #### 1. **Branching Strategy:**

Define a branching strategy that suits your project's needs. Common strategies include feature branching, git flow, and trunk-based development. Choose a strategy that balances isolation and integration. #### 2. **Pull Requests (PRs) or Merge Requests (MRs):**

Encourage developers to submit PRs or MRs for code changes. These requests allow for peer review, automated testing, and discussion before merging changes into the main codebase. #### 3. **Continuous Integration (CI):**

Implement CI pipelines that build, test, and analyze code changes automatically. CI ensures that code changes do not introduce regressions and conform to coding standards. #### 4. **Code Reviews:**

Conduct regular code reviews to maintain code quality and knowledge sharing. Tools like GitHub's code review features facilitate this process. #### 5. **Documentation and Guidelines:**

Maintain clear documentation and guidelines for using version control in your graphics project. Document branching conventions, PR/MR workflows, and coding standards. #### 6. **Collaboration Tools:**

Use collaboration tools such as issue trackers, project boards, and chat platforms (e.g., Slack, Discord) to coordinate tasks and communication among team members. #### 7. **Version Control Education:**

Ensure that all team members are familiar with the basics of version control. Provide training if necessary to improve the team's proficiency in using VCS effectively. #### 8. **Backup and Disaster Recovery:**

Implement backup and disaster recovery procedures for your version control system. This ensures that your code history remains secure and accessible. #### 9. **Code Ownership and Responsibilities:**

Clarify code ownership and responsibilities within the team. Define who is responsible for maintaining specific parts of the codebase to avoid conflicts.

In conclusion, version control is a fundamental tool for graphics programming projects. It enables effective collaboration, history tracking, and code quality control. Choosing the right VCS, defining collaboration strategies, and educating team members on best practices are essential steps to ensure smooth development in the world of graphics programming.

## Section 10.3: Documentation and Code Comments

Documentation and code comments play a crucial role in graphics programming projects. They help developers understand the codebase, facilitate collaboration, and ensure maintainability. In this section, we'll delve into the importance of documentation and provide guidelines for effective documentation practices. ### The Significance of Documentation 1. **Code Comprehension:** Graphics programming can be complex, involving intricate algorithms and optimizations. Documentation helps developers grasp the purpose and functionality of various components, making it easier to work with the codebase. 2. **Collaboration:** In a team environment, clear documentation becomes essential. It allows team members to understand each other's code and collaborate effectively. It also aids in onboarding new team members by providing context and guidance. 3. **Maintenance:** Graphics programs often evolve over time. Proper documentation ensures that developers can revisit and modify code confidently, even after an extended period. ### Types of Documentation 1. **Code**

**Comments:** Inline comments within the code provide immediate context. They explain the purpose of functions, variables, and complex algorithms. Use clear and concise comments to avoid confusion.

```
// Calculate the lighting intensity based on the
Lambertian reflection model.
float CalculateLightingIntensity(Vector3 normal,
Vector3 lightDirection) {
    // ... implementation details ...
}
```

2. **Function and Class Documentation:** Document functions and classes using comments or docstring-style comments. Describe the inputs, outputs, and behavior of functions and the purpose of classes.

```
/**
 * Represents a 3D vector in space.
 */
class Vector3 {
public:
    /**
     * Constructor to initialize the vector.
     * @param x X-component of the vector.
     * @param y Y-component of the vector.
     * @param z Z-component of the vector.
     */
    Vector3(float x, float y, float z) : x(x), y(y),
z(z) {}

    // ... other member functions ...
private:
    float x, y, z;
};
```

3. **File-Level Documentation:** At the top of each source file, provide a brief description of the file's purpose, its authors, and any relevant licensing information.

```
/**
 * @file renderer.cpp
 * @brief Implementation of the 3D graphics renderer.
```

```
 * @author John Doe
 * @date 2023-11-17
 * @license MIT License
 */
```

4. **API Documentation:** For libraries and APIs, maintain comprehensive documentation that includes usage examples, function descriptions, and version history. ### Documentation Guidelines

5. **Be Consistent:** Follow a consistent style for comments and documentation across the project. This makes it easier for developers to navigate and understand the code.

6. **Update Documentation:** Keep documentation up to date as the code evolves. Outdated documentation can be misleading and counterproductive.

7. **Use Descriptive Names:** Use meaningful variable, function, and class names. Well-named entities reduce the need for extensive comments.

8. **Explain Complex Logic:** When code contains complex algorithms or optimizations, include comments that explain the reasoning behind the approach.

9. **Consider Future Readers:** Write documentation with the assumption that someone else, or even your future self, will read and maintain the code.

10. **Use Documentation Tools:** Consider using documentation generation tools like Doxygen or Sphinx for large projects. These tools can automatically generate documentation from code comments.

In conclusion, documentation and code comments are essential for maintaining a graphics programming project. They enhance code comprehension, support collaboration, and ensure the long-term viability of the codebase. By following clear documentation practices and keeping comments up to date, developers can navigate complex graphics code with confidence.

# Section 10.4: Continuous Integration and Testing

Continuous Integration (CI) and Testing are fundamental aspects of any software development process, including graphics programming. They ensure that the codebase remains robust, functional, and free from regressions as it evolves. In this section, we will explore the importance of CI and testing in the context of graphics programming. ### The Significance of Continuous Integration

Continuous Integration is a development practice where code changes are automatically built, tested, and integrated into the project's main codebase. Here's why it's crucial: 1. **Early Issue Detection:** CI systems run automated tests whenever new code is submitted. This helps identify bugs and issues early in the development cycle, preventing them from becoming more significant problems. 2. **Integration Testing:** Graphics programs often rely on various components working together seamlessly. CI ensures that different parts of the code integrate correctly, avoiding unexpected compatibility issues. 3. **Regression Testing:** As the codebase grows, changes in one part of the code can unintentionally break other parts. CI systems run regression tests to catch these unintended consequences. 4. **Consistency:** CI promotes consistency by enforcing coding standards and build procedures across the team, reducing the likelihood of errors caused by inconsistent practices. ### Types of Testing in Graphics Programming 1. **Unit Testing:** Unit tests focus on individual functions or modules in isolation. In graphics programming, unit tests can validate critical algorithms, shaders, or rendering techniques. 2. **Integration Testing:** Integration tests verify that different components of the graphics pipeline work correctly together. For example, testing the interaction between shaders, rendering buffers, and the GPU. 3. **Functional Testing:** Functional tests evaluate the entire graphics application's functionality, often using predefined test scenarios. This ensures that the application performs as expected under various conditions. 4. **Performance Testing:** Graphics applications must run efficiently. Performance tests measure the application's speed, resource consumption, and responsiveness to ensure optimal performance. ### Implementing Continuous Integration

To implement CI in graphics programming, consider the following steps: 1. **Choose a CI Service:** Select a CI service like Travis CI, Jenkins, or GitHub Actions that integrates with your version control system. 2. **Automate the Build Process:** Create scripts or configuration files (e.g., using CMake) to automate the build process. This ensures that code can be compiled consistently across different environments. 3. **Write Tests:** Develop a comprehensive suite of tests that cover critical aspects of your graphics application. These tests should include unit, integration, functional, and performance tests. 4. **Version Control Integration:** Configure your CI service to trigger builds and tests whenever changes are pushed to the repository. 5. **Reporting and Notifications:** Set up reporting and notification mechanisms to alert the team when CI builds or tests fail. 6. **Continuous Deployment (Optional):** Consider integrating CI with your deployment process to automatically release tested code to production. ### Best Practices

Here are some best practices for CI and testing in graphics programming: 1. **Test Driven Development (TDD):** Consider adopting TDD practices, where tests are written before code. This can lead to more robust and testable code. 2. **Parallel Testing:** Utilize parallel testing to speed up the testing process, especially for performance tests that may take longer to run. 3. **Regular Maintenance:** Maintain and update your test suite as the code evolves. Ensure that tests remain relevant and cover new features. 4. **Code Coverage Analysis:** Monitor code coverage to identify areas that lack test coverage and address them accordingly.

In summary, Continuous Integration and Testing are essential practices in graphics programming to maintain code quality, prevent regressions, and ensure the overall reliability of your graphics application. By automating testing processes and integrating them into your development workflow, you can catch issues early and deliver a more stable and efficient product.

## Section 10.5: Keeping Up with Graphics API Updates

Staying up-to-date with the latest advancements and updates in graphics APIs is crucial for graphics programmers. Graphics APIs like OpenGL and Vulkan are continually evolving to provide better performance, new features, and improved capabilities. In this section, we will explore strategies and practices for keeping your graphics programming skills and projects current. ### The Importance of Keeping Up 1. **Performance Optimization:** New API versions often come with performance optimizations and enhancements. Staying current can lead to better rendering performance and efficiency in your applications. 2. **Access to New Features:** Graphics APIs introduce new features and functionalities with each update. These features can enable you to implement advanced rendering techniques and visual effects. 3. **Compatibility:** Over time, older API versions may become deprecated or unsupported. Keeping your knowledge and projects up-to-date ensures compatibility with modern hardware and software. 4. **Bug Fixes and Security:** Updates often include bug fixes and security patches, enhancing the stability and security of your applications. ### Strategies for Staying Current 1. **Documentation and Release Notes:** Regularly review the official documentation and release notes of the graphics API you are using. This provides insights into new features, changes, and deprecations. 2. **Online Communities:** Participate in online communities, forums, and discussion boards related to graphics programming. Engaging with fellow developers can help you stay informed about API updates and best practices. 3. **Tutorials and Courses:** Enroll in tutorials and online courses focused on graphics programming. Many platforms offer courses on the latest graphics APIs, helping you acquire new skills and knowledge. 4. **Sample Projects:** Study sample projects and open-source repositories that demonstrate the use of the latest API features. Analyzing code written by experienced developers can provide valuable insights. 5.

**Experimentation:** Create small test projects to experiment with new API features and techniques. Hands-on experience is one of the most effective ways to learn and adapt to changes. 6. **Conferences and Events:** Attend conferences, webinars, and events related to graphics programming. These gatherings often feature presentations and discussions on the latest trends and advancements. 7. **Books and Publications:** Read books and publications on graphics programming. Authors often update their content to reflect changes in the industry. ### Version Control and Backward Compatibility

When adopting new versions of graphics APIs, it's essential to consider backward compatibility. Here are some strategies: 1. **Version Control:** Use version control systems like Git to manage your codebase. This allows you to branch your project for experimentation without affecting the stable version. 2. **API Abstraction:** Consider using API abstraction libraries that provide a common interface to multiple graphics APIs. This can simplify the process of adapting your code to new APIs. 3. **Conditional Compilation:** Use conditional compilation to include code that targets specific API versions. This allows you to maintain compatibility with older versions while taking advantage of new features when available.

In conclusion, staying current with graphics API updates is vital for graphics programmers to harness the latest advancements, ensure compatibility, and optimize performance. By adopting the strategies mentioned above and maintaining a proactive approach to learning, you can continue to excel in the dynamic field of graphics programming.

# Chapter 11: Advanced Graphics Effects

## Section 11.1: Real-Time Ray Tracing

Real-time ray tracing is a cutting-edge graphics technique that has gained significant attention in recent years. Traditionally, rasterization-based rendering techniques have been the standard in real-time graphics, but ray tracing offers a more physically accurate way to simulate the behavior of light in a scene. In this section, we'll explore the fundamental concepts behind real-time ray tracing and how it differs from rasterization.

### Ray Tracing Basics

Ray tracing, at its core, simulates the behavior of light by tracing rays as they interact with objects in a scene. Each ray is cast from the camera's viewpoint into the scene and can potentially intersect with objects. When a ray intersects an object, various calculations are performed to determine how the ray interacts with the object's surface.

One of the key advantages of ray tracing is its ability to accurately simulate global illumination effects, such as reflections, refractions, and soft shadows. In a rasterization-based approach, achieving these effects can be challenging and often requires additional techniques and approximations.

### Real-Time Ray Tracing Hardware

To achieve real-time ray tracing, specialized hardware, such as ray tracing cores on modern GPUs, is essential. These dedicated cores accelerate ray-object intersection tests and other ray tracing calculations, making it feasible to trace a large number of rays in real-time.

### Ray Tracing Shaders

Ray tracing shaders are a crucial part of the real-time ray tracing pipeline. These shaders define how rays interact with objects in the scene. Ray generation shaders initiate the tracing process by casting rays from the camera. Intersection shaders determine if a ray intersects with an object, and closest hit shaders calculate the color and material properties of the object at the intersection point. Additionally, ray tracing shaders support features like transparency, reflections, and complex lighting models.

### Real-Time Ray Tracing in Games

Real-time ray tracing has found its way into video games, enhancing visual fidelity by providing realistic lighting and reflections. Games like Cyberpunk 2077 and Minecraft have incorporated ray tracing to create immersive environments with stunning lighting effects. However, the computational demands of real-time ray tracing still pose challenges, and optimizations are continuously developed to achieve higher performance.

In the next sections, we will delve deeper into the specific aspects of real-time ray tracing, including ray-object intersection algorithms, acceleration structures, and the integration of ray tracing into existing rendering pipelines. Understanding these concepts is crucial for harnessing the power of real-time ray tracing in graphics programming.

## Section 11.2: Global Illumination Techniques

Global illumination (GI) techniques are an essential component of advanced graphics effects, aiming to simulate how light interacts with the environment realistically. While GI encompasses various methods, we'll explore some of the key techniques commonly used in computer graphics. ### Ray Tracing-Based GI

Real-time ray tracing, as discussed in the previous section, plays a pivotal role in achieving realistic global illumination. Ray tracing techniques like path tracing, photon mapping, and radiosity solve the complex problem of simulating how light bounces and interacts with surfaces in a scene. #### Path Tracing

Path tracing is a Monte Carlo ray tracing method that simulates the transport of light in a scene. It traces rays from the camera into the scene, and for each ray, it samples materials and calculates how light is absorbed, reflected, and refracted. By tracing a large number of paths and averaging their contributions, path tracing can simulate indirect lighting, soft shadows, and complex light transport effects. #### Photon Mapping

Photon mapping is another global illumination technique that focuses on simulating indirect lighting. It involves two main passes: the photon tracing pass and the radiance estimation pass. During photon tracing, photons are emitted from light sources and stored in a photon map. In the radiance estimation pass, rays from the camera search the photon map to estimate radiance values for each pixel. Photon mapping is particularly well-suited for handling caustics and other complex lighting effects. #### Radiosity

Radiosity is a GI technique that focuses on the interaction of surfaces within a scene. It models how surfaces emit, reflect, and transmit light. Radiosity methods divide the scene into small patches and compute the amount of light exchanged between them. Radiosity can simulate diffuse inter-reflections accurately but may require precomputation for complex scenes. ### Screen Space Techniques

While ray tracing-based GI techniques offer high-quality results, they can be computationally intensive. To achieve real-time performance in games, screen-space techniques are often employed. #### Screen Space Ambient Occlusion (SSAO)

SSAO is a screen-space technique that approximates ambient occlusion, which helps to simulate contact shadows and occluded lighting. It works by sampling nearby pixels in the depth buffer to determine how occluded each point on the screen is. SSAO is a cost-effective way to improve the realism of a scene's lighting. #### Screen Space Reflections (SSR)

SSR is used to simulate reflections in real-time graphics. It works by ray tracing reflections in screen space, considering the depth and material properties of surfaces. While SSR can produce convincing results, it may exhibit limitations in handling complex scenes with multiple reflective surfaces. ### Hybrid Approaches

In practice, a combination of techniques is often used to balance realism and performance. Hybrid approaches may use ray tracing for primary visibility and screen-space techniques to enhance specific lighting effects. The choice of GI technique depends on the project's requirements and the available hardware.

Understanding global illumination techniques and how to implement them is crucial for graphics programmers aiming to achieve realistic lighting and reflections in their applications. The choice of technique depends on the desired level of visual fidelity and the computational resources available.

## Section 11.3: Procedural Generation of Textures

Procedural generation is a powerful technique in computer graphics that allows for the creation of textures and content algorithmically rather than relying on manually authored assets. Procedural textures are generated mathematically, providing a high level of flexibility and enabling the creation of diverse and unique textures. In this section, we'll explore the concept of procedural generation and its application to texture creation. ### What Is Procedural Generation?

Procedural generation involves using algorithms and mathematical functions to create content, such as textures, terrain, or 3D models, at runtime. It offers several advantages, including the ability to create infinite variations of content, reduce storage requirements, and adapt content based on runtime parameters. #### Noise Functions

One of the fundamental building blocks of procedural generation is noise functions. These functions generate random-like patterns that are coherent and deterministic. Common noise functions include Perlin noise, Simplex noise, and Worley noise. These noise functions serve as the basis for creating various textures. ### Procedural Texture Generation

Procedural texture generation involves creating textures by combining and manipulating noise functions and other mathematical operations. Here are some commonly used techniques: #### Perlin and Simplex Noise

Perlin and Simplex noise are often used to create organic-looking textures, such as clouds, marble, or terrain. By modulating the noise values and adjusting parameters, you can create a wide range of textures, from natural landscapes to abstract patterns. #### Fractal Patterns

Fractal patterns, generated using techniques like fractal brownian motion (fBm), can produce complex and detailed textures. These textures exhibit self-similarity at different scales, making them suitable for simulating natural phenomena like rock surfaces, forests, or turbulence. #### Procedural Noise Textures

Procedural noise textures, like wood grain, marble, or granite, are commonly used in 3D rendering. By applying mathematical operations to noise functions, you can control the appearance of these textures, including their color, roughness, and scale. ### Seamless Textures

One challenge in procedural texture generation is creating seamless textures that can be tiled without visible seams. Techniques such as wrapping and blending the edges of textures or using seamless noise functions are employed to achieve this. ### Applications of Procedural Textures

Procedural textures find applications in various fields, including computer games, movies, and architectural visualization. They are used for creating terrain, simulating natural elements like fire and smoke, and generating realistic materials like rust, wood, or fabric. ### Implementation

The implementation of procedural texture generation depends on the graphics API or engine being used. Many graphics APIs provide built-in support for shader-based procedural texture generation. Below is a simplified example of generating Perlin noise in GLSL (OpenGL Shading Language):

```glsl
// Perlin noise function
float noise(vec2 p) {
    return fract(sin(dot(p, vec2(12.9898, 78.233))) *
43758.5453);
}

void main() {
```

```
    vec2 uv = gl_FragCoord.xy / u_resolution;
    float value = noise(uv * 10.0);
    gl_FragColor = vec4(value, value, value, 1.0);
}
```

This shader generates Perlin noise and assigns it to the pixel color, creating a grayscale procedural texture.

Procedural generation is a valuable technique for creating textures that are versatile, efficient, and can add realism to computer graphics. Understanding noise functions and procedural texture generation opens up possibilities for creating a wide range of visual effects and materials.

## Section 11.4: Advanced Post-Processing Effects

Post-processing effects play a crucial role in enhancing the visual quality and realism of computer graphics. These effects are applied to the rendered image after the scene has been rendered and are often used to simulate real-world phenomena, correct rendering artifacts, and achieve artistic styles. In this section, we'll delve into advanced post-processing effects commonly used in graphics programming. ### Bloom

Bloom is a popular post-processing effect used to simulate the perception of intense light sources. It creates a halo or "bloom" around bright areas in the scene, making them appear more vibrant and realistic. Bloom is achieved through a multi-pass rendering technique.

In the first pass, a bright pass is rendered, where only the brightest pixels in the scene are extracted using a threshold. Then, this bright pass is blurred using a Gaussian blur filter to create the bloom effect. Finally, the original scene and the bloom pass are combined to produce the final result.

Here's a simplified GLSL shader example for implementing a basic bloom effect:

```
// Bright pass fragment shader
void main() {
```

```
    vec4 color = texture2D(u_inputTexture,
v_texCoords);
    float luminance = dot(color.rgb, vec3(0.2126,
0.7152, 0.0722));
    if (luminance > u_threshold) {
        gl_FragColor = color;
    } else {
        gl_FragColor = vec4(0.0);
    }
}
```

## Depth of Field

Depth of field (DOF) is a post-processing effect that simulates the way camera lenses focus on objects at a specific depth while blurring objects at other depths. It is commonly used in 3D rendering to create more realistic and cinematic visuals.

DOF is achieved by calculating the depth of each pixel in the scene and then applying a blur based on the difference between the pixel's depth and the focal depth. The result is a visually pleasing blurring effect that mimics the behavior of real cameras.

### Motion Blur

Motion blur is another post-processing effect that simulates the blurring of fast-moving objects in a scene. It adds a sense of motion and realism to animations and games. Motion blur can be implemented by rendering multiple intermediate frames between the current and previous frames and then blending them together to create the blurred effect.

### Ambient Occlusion

Ambient occlusion (AO) is a shading technique used to simulate the soft shadows that occur in areas where objects are close together and block ambient light. AO is crucial for adding depth and realism to 3D scenes.

In post-processing, screen-space ambient occlusion (SSAO) is a common technique. It works by sampling the depth buffer to detect nearby surfaces and then darkens pixels that are occluded or hidden from ambient light. The result is a subtle darkening

effect in crevices and corners, enhancing the perception of depth.
### Chromatic Aberration

Chromatic aberration is a visual effect that simulates the dispersion of light in camera lenses, causing color fringing around the edges of objects. While it is often considered an optical defect, it is sometimes used artistically to create a retro or surreal look in graphics.

Chromatic aberration can be implemented by offsetting the RGB channels of the rendered image based on their wavelength. This effect is usually subtle but can be adjusted for different artistic styles. ### Implementation and Optimization

The implementation of advanced post-processing effects often involves multiple rendering passes and the use of framebuffers. While these effects can greatly enhance visuals, they can also be computationally expensive. Therefore, optimization techniques such as downsampling, mipmapping, and shader optimizations are essential to maintain real-time performance.

In conclusion, advanced post-processing effects are powerful tools in graphics programming that can significantly impact the visual quality and style of rendered scenes. Understanding the techniques and algorithms behind these effects is essential for creating compelling and immersive graphics experiences.

## Section 11.5: VR and AR Integration

Virtual Reality (VR) and Augmented Reality (AR) are transformative technologies that have revolutionized the way we interact with digital content and the real world. In this section, we will explore the integration of graphics programming with VR and AR systems, allowing for immersive and interactive experiences. ### Virtual Reality (VR) #### VR Headsets and Tracking

VR experiences rely on specialized headsets that provide users with a fully immersive 3D environment. These headsets are equipped with motion sensors, accelerometers, and gyroscopes to track the user's head movements accurately. This tracking data is crucial for updating the view in real-time to match the user's perspective, creating a sense of presence within the virtual environment.

Modern VR headsets, like the Oculus Rift and HTC Vive, offer high-resolution displays, low-latency tracking, and hand controllers for natural interaction. Developers can access tracking data and user input through SDKs provided by headset manufacturers.

#### VR Rendering Techniques

To create realistic VR experiences, graphics programmers must consider factors such as frame rate, stereoscopic rendering, and user comfort. Achieving a high and consistent frame rate is essential to prevent motion sickness and ensure a smooth experience.

Stereoscopic rendering involves rendering two slightly different views—one for each eye—to create the illusion of depth. This technique requires careful calibration to match the user's interpupillary distance (IPD) and maintain accurate depth perception.

#### Interaction and Controllers in VR

VR experiences often involve hand controllers or tracked motion controllers. These devices allow users to interact with objects in the virtual world, making VR applications more engaging and intuitive. Developers can map controller inputs to in-game actions and physics simulations, providing users with a high degree of interactivity.

### Augmented Reality (AR)

#### AR Displays and Sensors

Augmented Reality enhances the real-world environment with digital information and objects. AR systems use displays such as smartphones, tablets, smart glasses, or dedicated AR headsets to overlay computer-generated content onto the user's view of the physical world. These devices may include cameras, depth sensors, and GPS for tracking and scene understanding.

#### Marker-Based and Markerless AR

AR applications can use markers, which are physical objects or patterns recognized by the AR system, as anchors for digital content. Markerless AR, on the other hand, relies on computer vision techniques to detect and track features in the real world, enabling content placement on arbitrary surfaces. #### Integrating Graphics with Real-World Environments

One of the key challenges in AR graphics programming is aligning digital objects with the real world seamlessly. This involves spatial tracking, object recognition, and occlusion handling. AR frameworks and SDKs, like ARKit (iOS) and ARCore (Android), provide tools for developers to anchor and manipulate virtual objects within the user's surroundings. ### Challenges and Considerations in VR and AR Graphics

Integrating graphics programming with VR and AR introduces unique challenges. Achieving low latency, high frame rates, and accurate tracking is critical to providing a comfortable and immersive experience. Additionally, developers must consider user interface design, gesture recognition, and accessibility to ensure that AR and VR applications are user-friendly.

In conclusion, VR and AR integration in graphics programming opens up exciting possibilities for immersive and interactive experiences. Whether creating VR games, AR navigation apps, or industrial training simulations, graphics programmers play a vital role in shaping the future of these technologies, making them more accessible and compelling for users worldwide.

# Chapter 12: Graphics and Game Engines

Graphics and game engines are the backbone of modern video games and interactive applications. In this chapter, we'll delve into the world of engines and explore how they utilize graphics programming to create immersive and interactive experiences. ### Section 12.1: Overview of Game Engines

Game engines are software frameworks designed to simplify and streamline the development of video games and interactive applications. They provide a wide range of tools, libraries, and features that help developers create, render, and manage game content efficiently. Let's take a closer look at the key aspects of game engines. #### Game Logic and Scripting

Game engines typically offer scripting support that allows developers to define game logic, behaviors, and interactions. Scripting languages like Lua or Python are commonly used for this purpose. Game designers and developers can use scripts to control character movements, trigger events, and create complex gameplay mechanics. #### Asset Management

Game engines excel at managing various types of digital assets, including 3D models, textures, audio files, and animations. These assets are organized and stored in a way that makes it easy for developers to import, manipulate, and integrate them into the game. Asset pipelines and import/export tools are often part of the engine's feature set. #### Rendering and Graphics

Graphics programming plays a central role in game engines. They are responsible for rendering 2D and 3D graphics, managing rendering pipelines, and optimizing performance. Engines often provide rendering APIs and shader systems that allow developers to create visually stunning effects and optimize rendering performance. #### Physics Simulation

Many game engines include built-in physics simulation engines that handle realistic interactions between objects in the game world. This includes simulating gravity, collisions, ragdoll physics, and more. Physics engines enable the creation of dynamic and immersive gameplay experiences. #### Audio and Sound

Sound and audio are essential components of game development. Game engines often include audio systems that handle spatial audio, background music, sound effects, and more. Developers can use these systems to create immersive audio experiences that enhance gameplay. #### Cross-Platform Support

Game engines are designed to support multiple platforms, including Windows, macOS, Linux, consoles, mobile devices, and more. This allows developers to target a wide range of platforms with a single codebase, making game development more accessible and cost-effective. #### Game Editor

Most game engines come with a game editor or development environment that provides a visual interface for designing game levels, scenes, and assets. Game designers can use these editors to create, edit, and test game content without writing code. #### Scripting APIs

Game engines expose scripting APIs that allow developers to extend and customize engine functionality. This enables the creation of custom gameplay mechanics, AI behaviors, and tools tailored to the specific needs of a game project. #### Networking and Multiplayer

For multiplayer and online games, engines often include networking capabilities that facilitate communication between players, servers, and game clients. These features enable the development of online multiplayer games and collaborative experiences.

In summary, game engines are versatile tools that empower developers to create interactive and visually stunning applications. Graphics programming is a fundamental part of game engine development, enabling the rendering of captivating visuals and the optimization of performance. In the following sections of this chapter, we will explore how graphics and game engines leverage graphics programming to create engaging and immersive gaming experiences.

## Section 12.2: Integrating OpenGL and Vulkan with Engines

Game engines often incorporate graphics APIs like OpenGL and Vulkan to handle rendering tasks efficiently. These APIs provide the necessary tools for creating and rendering 2D and 3D graphics, which are essential for game development. In this section, we will explore how engines integrate OpenGL and Vulkan into their architecture. ### Engine Graphics Abstraction

Game engines abstract the underlying graphics APIs to provide a unified interface for developers. This abstraction layer shields developers from the low-level intricacies of OpenGL or Vulkan, making it easier to work with graphics in a cross-platform manner.

The engine's graphics abstraction typically includes components like rendering pipelines, shader management, texture loading, and model rendering. This abstraction allows developers to write code that targets the engine's graphics API rather than dealing directly with OpenGL or Vulkan. ### OpenGL Integration

For engines that use OpenGL, integration involves setting up OpenGL contexts, managing OpenGL resources, and providing high-level abstractions for rendering tasks. OpenGL is widely supported across various platforms, making it a popular choice for engine developers.

Engine developers often create OpenGL renderers that encapsulate OpenGL-specific functionality. These renderers are responsible for translating the engine's rendering commands into OpenGL calls. They handle tasks such as rendering models, applying shaders, and managing textures. ### Vulkan Integration

In contrast, Vulkan integration is more complex due to its low-level nature. Vulkan provides fine-grained control over GPU resources and parallel execution of rendering tasks. Engine developers need to create Vulkan renderers that orchestrate the entire rendering process.

Vulkan renderers are responsible for tasks like command buffer creation, pipeline setup, and resource management. Vulkan's explicit nature requires developers to be meticulous in managing resources, synchronization, and memory allocation.

The advantage of Vulkan integration lies in its potential for superior performance and efficiency. It allows developers to optimize rendering pipelines and minimize CPU-GPU synchronization, resulting in smoother and more responsive graphics. ### Cross-Platform Considerations

Game engines aim to be cross-platform, meaning they can run on various operating systems and hardware configurations. To achieve this, engine developers must ensure that their OpenGL or Vulkan integration is robust and compatible across platforms.

Cross-platform considerations include dealing with platform-specific issues, graphics driver differences, and ensuring that the engine can adapt to the capabilities of the target hardware. Engine developers often rely on libraries and tools that abstract platform-specific details, such as GLFW for window management and MoltenVK for Vulkan on macOS. ### Graphics API Switching

Some engines offer the flexibility to switch between different graphics APIs, such as OpenGL, Vulkan, or DirectX, at runtime. This allows developers to choose the API that best suits their target platforms or take advantage of specific features.

To implement API switching, engines must provide a common interface for rendering tasks and create separate backend implementations for each API. Developers can then select the desired API when configuring the engine for a particular project.

In summary, game engines play a pivotal role in simplifying graphics programming by abstracting the complexities of OpenGL or Vulkan. They provide high-level abstractions that enable developers to focus on creating compelling gameplay and visuals while ensuring compatibility across diverse platforms. Whether using OpenGL for its ease of use or Vulkan for its performance advantages, engine integration with these graphics APIs is essential for delivering immersive gaming experiences.

## Section 12.3: Developing a Simple Game Engine

Developing a game engine is a complex and challenging task, but it can be highly rewarding for those who want full control over their game's technology stack. In this section, we'll explore the process of developing a simple game engine, highlighting key components and considerations. ### Engine Architecture

A game engine is a software framework that provides various services to simplify game development. It typically consists of several core modules: 1. **Rendering Engine** : Responsible for graphics rendering, including handling shaders, textures, and 3D models. In our simple engine, we may use OpenGL for rendering. 2. **Physics Engine** : Manages physics simulations, collisions, and interactions between game objects. 3. **Audio Engine** : Handles audio playback, sound effects, and music. 4. **Input Handling** : Manages user input from devices like keyboards, mice, and game controllers. 5. **Scene Management** : Organizes game objects, scenes, and levels. 6. **Resource Management** : Loads and manages assets like textures, models, and audio files. 7. **Scripting and Logic** : Allows developers to define game behavior using scripts or a scripting language. 8. **Game Logic** : Implements game-specific rules and logic, such as scoring, enemy behavior, and win/lose conditions. 9. **User Interface (UI)** : Renders and manages the game's user interface elements. ### Rendering with OpenGL

For our simple game engine, we'll focus on the rendering engine and use OpenGL as the graphics API. OpenGL provides a versatile and cross-platform way to render 2D and 3D graphics. #### Initializing OpenGL

To begin, we need to initialize OpenGL by creating a rendering context and setting up basic rendering parameters. This typically involves configuring OpenGL version, creating a window using a library like GLFW, and setting up a rendering loop.

```
// Initialize GLFW
glfwInit();
```

```c
// Configure GLFW
glfwWindowHint(GLFW_CONTEXT_VERSION_MAJOR, 3);
glfwWindowHint(GLFW_CONTEXT_VERSION_MINOR, 3);
glfwWindowHint(GLFW_OPENGL_PROFILE,
GLFW_OPENGL_CORE_PROFILE);

// Create a windowed mode window and its OpenGL context
GLFWwindow* window = glfwCreateWindow(800, 600, "Simple
Game Engine", NULL, NULL);
if (!window) {
    glfwTerminate();
    return -1;
}

// Make the window's context current
glfwMakeContextCurrent(window);
```

*Rendering a Triangle*

To demonstrate rendering with OpenGL, let's render a simple triangle:

```c
float vertices[] = {
    -0.5f, -0.5f, 0.0f,
     0.5f, -0.5f, 0.0f,
     0.0f,  0.5f, 0.0f
};

unsigned int VBO, VAO;
glGenVertexArrays(1, &VAO);
glGenBuffers(1, &VBO);

// Bind Vertex Array Object
glBindVertexArray(VAO);

// Bind and set vertex buffer(s)
glBindBuffer(GL_ARRAY_BUFFER, VBO);
glBufferData(GL_ARRAY_BUFFER, sizeof(vertices),
vertices, GL_STATIC_DRAW);

// Set vertex attribute pointers
```

```
glVertexAttribPointer(0, 3, GL_FLOAT, GL_FALSE, 3 *
sizeof(float), (void*)0);
glEnableVertexAttribArray(0);

// Render Loop
while (!glfwWindowShouldClose(window)) {
    // ...

    // Render the triangle
    glUseProgram(shaderProgram);
    glBindVertexArray(VAO);
    glDrawArrays(GL_TRIANGLES, 0, 3);

    // ...

    // Swap front and back buffers
    glfwSwapBuffers(window);

    // Poll for and process events
    glfwPollEvents();
}

// Cleanup
glDeleteVertexArrays(1, &VAO);
glDeleteBuffers(1, &VBO);
```

This code sets up a basic OpenGL context, creates a triangle's vertex data, and renders it using a simple rendering loop. In a real game engine, rendering would be much more complex, supporting multiple objects, materials, and shaders. ### Extending the Engine

Developing a full-fledged game engine involves implementing the various modules mentioned earlier and integrating them seamlessly. The engine's architecture should allow developers to create and manipulate game objects, define behaviors, and manage resources efficiently.

While this simple engine serves as a starting point, real-world engines like Unity or Unreal Engine are far more sophisticated, offering extensive toolsets and features for game development. Building a game engine from scratch is a significant undertaking and often requires a team of experienced developers. However, it can be a valuable learning experience and a path to creating highly customized games with full creative control.

## Section 12.4: Physics Simulation in Games

Physics simulation is a critical aspect of many games, as it enables realistic interactions between game objects and environments. In this section, we'll explore the fundamental concepts of physics simulation in game engines and how it contributes to immersive gameplay experiences. ### Rigid Body Dynamics

Rigid body dynamics is a common approach to simulating physical objects in games. In this context, a rigid body is an object that maintains its shape and size while moving and interacting with other objects. Rigid body physics involve simulating the motion, collisions, and forces applied to these objects.

Key components of rigid body dynamics include: 1. **Mass** : Each rigid body has a mass value, which determines how it responds to forces. Heavier objects require more force to accelerate or move. 2. **Forces** : Forces such as gravity, friction, and user input (e.g., player-controlled movement) affect the motion of rigid bodies. 3. **Collisions** : Detecting and resolving collisions between rigid bodies is crucial for realistic physics simulation. Collision detection algorithms determine when and where collisions occur, while collision response algorithms handle the resulting interactions. 4. **Integration** : Numerical integration methods like Euler's method or Verlet integration are used to update the positions and velocities of rigid bodies over time. 5. **Constraints** : Constraints are used to maintain object relationships, like joints between connected objects or constraints that prevent objects from passing through each other. 6. **Friction** : Friction models simulate how objects resist sliding against each other. Friction

coefficients control the strength of frictional forces. ###
Implementing Physics Simulation

Here's a simplified example of implementing basic physics
simulation for a simple 2D game:

```python
class RigidBody:
    def __init__(self, mass):
        self.mass = mass
        self.position = Vector2(0, 0)  # Initial
position
        self.velocity = Vector2(0, 0)  # Initial
velocity
        self.forces = Vector2(0, 0)    # Forces applied
to the object

    def apply_force(self, force):
        self.forces += force

    def update(self, delta_time):
        # Calculate acceleration based on forces and
mass
        acceleration = self.forces / self.mass

        # Update velocity using Euler integration
        self.velocity += acceleration * delta_time

        # Update position using the new velocity
        self.position += self.velocity * delta_time

        # Clear forces for the next frame
        self.forces = Vector2(0, 0)

# Example usage:
ball = RigidBody(mass=1.0)
gravity = Vector2(0, -9.81)  # Acceleration due to
gravity

# Apply gravity as a force
ball.apply_force(gravity)
```

```
# In the game loop:
delta_time = 0.016  # Example time step
ball.update(delta_time)
```

In this Python example, we have a `RigidBody` class that represents a simple rigid body with mass, position, velocity, and forces. We apply forces, like gravity, to the object and update its position and velocity over time using Euler integration. While this is a basic example, real game engines use more sophisticated physics libraries and algorithms to handle complex interactions.
### Physics Engines

Many game engines incorporate physics engines like NVIDIA PhysX, Bullet, or Havok to handle complex physics simulations. These engines provide pre-built solutions for rigid body dynamics, soft body dynamics, cloth simulation, vehicle physics, and more. Integrating a physics engine into a game engine allows developers to focus on gameplay and content creation while leveraging advanced physics simulation capabilities.

In summary, physics simulation is a vital component of game engines, enabling realistic and engaging gameplay experiences. Whether through basic rigid body dynamics or advanced physics engines, it plays a crucial role in creating interactive and immersive worlds in video games.

## Section 12.5: Audio and Sound in Games

Audio and sound are integral components of video games, enhancing immersion and gameplay experiences. In this section, we'll delve into the importance of audio in games, various audio technologies, and techniques for implementing sound in game development. ### The Importance of Audio

Audio plays a significant role in shaping a player's emotional connection to a game. It contributes to the game's atmosphere, storytelling, and feedback mechanisms. Here are some key aspects of audio in games: 1. **Immersive Environments** : Ambient sounds, music, and sound effects transport players to the game world, making it feel more immersive. 2. **Storytelling** :

Dialogues, voiceovers, and narrative-driven audio help convey the game's story and characters. 3. **Feedback and Cues** : Sound cues provide crucial feedback, indicating actions, danger, achievements, and progress. For example, footsteps, gunshots, or health pickups. 4. **Emotional Impact** : Music and sound can evoke emotions and set the mood. Tense music during a boss fight or cheerful tunes in a victory sequence influence the player's emotional state. 5. **Accessibility** : Audio cues can be essential for players with visual impairments, making games more accessible. ### Audio Technologies in Games

Game developers use various audio technologies and tools to create immersive soundscapes. Some common elements include: 1. **Digital Audio Workstations (DAWs)** : DAWs like Pro Tools, Logic Pro, or Ableton Live are used to create and edit music and sound effects. 2. **Sound Libraries** : Developers often leverage sound libraries containing pre-recorded or synthesized sounds for quick access to a wide range of audio assets. 3. **Audio Middleware** : Middleware solutions like FMOD and Wwise provide tools for interactive audio design, spatial audio, and dynamic soundtracks. 4. **3D Audio** : In modern games, 3D audio technology allows sounds to originate from specific locations in the game world, creating a more realistic auditory experience. ### Implementing Sound in Games

Here's a simplified example of how sound effects can be implemented in a game using a popular game engine like Unity:

```
using UnityEngine;

public class AudioManager : MonoBehaviour
{
    public AudioClip jumpSound;
    public AudioClip coinCollectSound;

    private AudioSource audioSource;

    private void Start()
    {
        audioSource = GetComponent<AudioSource>();
```

```
    }

    public void PlayJumpSound()
    {
        audioSource.PlayOneShot(jumpSound);
    }

    public void PlayCoinCollectSound()
    {
        audioSource.PlayOneShot(coinCollectSound);
    }
}
```

In this Unity script, an `AudioManager` component is attached to a GameObject. It has references to audio clips for jump and coin collection sounds. The `PlayJumpSound` and `PlayCoinCollectSound` methods trigger the respective sound effects when called. This is a simple example, and in larger games, more complex audio systems and state management would be implemented. ### Considerations for Audio Design

Effective audio design in games involves considerations like spatial audio, dynamic mixing, and adaptive soundtracks. Additionally, game developers must optimize audio assets to reduce memory and CPU usage.

In summary, audio and sound are critical components of modern video games, contributing to immersion, storytelling, and gameplay feedback. Game developers use various audio technologies and tools to create engaging soundscapes, enhancing the overall gaming experience for players.

## Chapter 13: 2D Graphics and GUI Development

In this chapter, we'll explore the world of 2D graphics and Graphical User Interface (GUI) development within the context of graphics programming. While much of the previous content focused on 3D graphics and low-level graphics APIs like OpenGL and Vulkan, 2D graphics and GUIs have their unique challenges and applications. ### Section 13.1: Building 2D Games with OpenGL and Vulkan

2D games remain popular across various platforms, from mobile devices to desktop computers. While dedicated 2D game engines exist, some developers prefer to use low-level graphics APIs like OpenGL and Vulkan for the flexibility and control they offer. #### Benefits of Using OpenGL and Vulkan for 2D Games 1. **Performance** : OpenGL and Vulkan provide excellent performance, even for 2D rendering. They allow developers to make efficient use of hardware acceleration. 2. **Cross-Platform** : Many games target multiple platforms. By using OpenGL or Vulkan, you can write code that works across different operating systems and devices. 3. **Customization** : Low-level APIs offer more customization options. You can implement unique rendering effects and optimizations tailored to your game. 4. **Learning Opportunity** : If you're already familiar with OpenGL or Vulkan from 3D development, leveraging the same API for 2D can be efficient. #### Basic Setup for 2D Rendering

To get started with 2D rendering using OpenGL or Vulkan, you'll need to set up your rendering context and initialize your game window. Here's a simplified example using OpenGL in C++ with the popular library GLFW:

```cpp
#include <GL/glew.h>
#include <GLFW/glfw3.h>

int main() {
    // Initialize GLFW
    if (!glfwInit()) {
        // Handle initialization failure
        return -1;
    }

    // Create a windowed mode window and its OpenGL context
    GLFWwindow* window = glfwCreateWindow(800, 600, "2D Game", NULL, NULL);
    if (!window) {
```

```
        // Handle window creation failure
        glfwTerminate();
        return -1;
    }

    // Make the window's context current
    glfwMakeContextCurrent(window);

    // Initialize GLEW to access OpenGL functions
    if (glewInit() != GLEW_OK) {
        // Handle GLEW initialization failure
        return -1;
    }

    // Main game loop
    while (!glfwWindowShouldClose(window)) {
        // Render your 2D scene here

        // Swap front and back buffers
        glfwSwapBuffers(window);

        // Poll for and process events
        glfwPollEvents();
    }

    // Terminate GLFW
    glfwTerminate();

    return 0;
}
```

This code initializes GLFW, creates a window, sets up an OpenGL context, and enters a main game loop for rendering. #### 2D Rendering Techniques

Once your 2D game is set up, you can employ various rendering techniques, such as: - **Sprites** : Rendering 2D textures or sprites onto the screen. - **Tilemaps** : Building game environments using tile-based maps. - **Text Rendering** : Displaying text and fonts. - **GUI Elements** : Creating buttons, menus, and HUD elements.

Additionally, you can implement 2D physics and collision detection, animations, and user input handling to create a complete 2D game experience.

In the subsequent sections of this chapter, we'll delve deeper into specific aspects of 2D graphics and GUI development, including GUI design and implementation, user input handling, animations, debugging, and profiling.

## Section 13.2: GUI Design and Implementation

Graphical User Interfaces (GUIs) are essential components of many applications, from software tools to video games. A well-designed GUI enhances user experience and simplifies interaction with the application. In this section, we'll explore the principles of GUI design and discuss how to implement GUIs in the context of 2D graphics programming using OpenGL or Vulkan. ### Principles of GUI Design

Before diving into implementation, it's crucial to understand the fundamental principles of GUI design: 1. **User-Centered Design** : Start by considering the needs and preferences of your target users. The GUI should be intuitive and user-friendly. 2. **Consistency** : Maintain a consistent visual style and layout throughout the GUI. Consistency aids in navigation and reduces cognitive load. 3. **Hierarchy and Organization** : Organize GUI elements hierarchically. Important actions or information should be more prominent and easily accessible. 4. **Feedback** : Provide immediate feedback for user actions. Visual cues, such as changing button colors when clicked, help users understand the interface's response. 5. **Simplicity** : Keep the GUI simple and clutter-free. Avoid unnecessary elements or features that can confuse users. 6. **Visual Design** : Pay attention to aesthetics. Use appropriate colors, typography, and visual elements to create an appealing interface. ### Implementing GUIs with OpenGL or Vulkan

To implement GUIs with OpenGL or Vulkan, you can use a combination of techniques, such as rendering textures, text, and simple geometric shapes. Here are some key considerations: 1. **Texture Rendering** : Create and load textures for GUI elements like buttons, icons, and backgrounds. OpenGL and Vulkan support texture mapping, allowing you to display these textures on quads or rectangles. 2. **Text Rendering** : Implement text rendering for displaying labels, instructions, or user input. Libraries like FreeType can help render text efficiently. 3. **Layout System** : Develop a layout system to position and size GUI elements. Consider using a grid-based or relative layout approach for flexibility. 4. **User Interaction** : Implement event handling for user interactions like mouse clicks, keyboard input, and touch gestures. Map these inputs to GUI actions. 5. **Widgets and Controls** : Create reusable GUI widgets and controls like buttons, checkboxes, sliders, and text input fields. These can be encapsulated as classes or functions. 6. **State Management** : Maintain the state of GUI elements, such as whether a button is pressed or a checkbox is checked. Update the GUI accordingly based on these states.

Here's a simplified example of creating a button widget using OpenGL in C++:

```cpp
class Button {
public:
    Button(float x, float y, float width, float height,
const char* text)
        : position(x, y), size(width, height),
label(text) {}

    void render() {
        // Render the button background quad with a
texture
        // Render the label text
    }

    bool isClicked(float mouseX, float mouseY) {
        // Check if the mouse coordinates are within
the button's boundaries
        // Return true if clicked, false otherwise
    }
```

```
private:
    glm::vec2 position;
    glm::vec2 size;
    std::string label;
    // Other button-related data
};
```

This code defines a simple `Button` class that encapsulates rendering and interaction logic.

In the subsequent sections of this chapter, we'll explore user input handling in 2D games, animations and transitions for GUI elements, and techniques for debugging and profiling 2D graphics applications.

## Section 13.3: User Input Handling in 2D Games

In 2D game development, handling user input is a fundamental aspect of creating interactive and engaging experiences. Whether you're developing a platformer, puzzle game, or any other type of 2D game, effective input handling is crucial. In this section, we'll explore various aspects of user input handling in 2D games. ### Types of User Input

User input in 2D games can come from various sources, including: 1. **Keyboard Input** : Keyboard input is commonly used for actions such as character movement, menu navigation, and triggering abilities. Most game engines provide mechanisms for detecting key presses and releases. 2. **Mouse Input** : The mouse can be used for aiming, interacting with on-screen elements, and navigating menus. Detecting mouse clicks, movement, and position is essential. 3. **Touch Input** : For mobile games and touch-enabled devices, touch input is crucial. Handling touch events like taps, swipes, and multi-touch gestures enhances the gameplay experience. 4. **Game Controllers** : Gamepads and controllers are often used for console games and can also be supported in PC games. Handling controller input involves mapping buttons and analog sticks to in-game actions. ### Input Handling Strategies

Efficient and responsive input handling is vital for creating a seamless gaming experience. Here are some strategies for handling user input in 2D games: 1. **Input Polling** : In this approach, you continuously check the state of input devices (e.g., keys, mouse, or touch) during each game frame. You maintain a record of which keys or buttons are pressed and act accordingly. 2. **Event-Based Input** : Event-driven input systems use callbacks or events to handle user input. When a key is pressed or a mouse click occurs, an event is triggered, and you respond to that event with specific actions. 3. **Input Buffers** : Input buffering involves storing input events in a queue and processing them one by one. This can help prevent input loss and ensure that all user actions are processed. 4. **Action Mapping** : Rather than directly checking for specific keys or buttons, you can create an action mapping system. Define in-game actions (e.g., "Jump," "Shoot") and map them to various input sources. This abstraction simplifies input handling. ### Example Input Handling in Unity (C#)

In Unity, a popular game engine, you can handle user input using the Input class. Here's a simplified example of handling keyboard input in C#:

```
void Update() {
    // Check if the "Jump" key (e.g., Spacebar) is
pressed
    if (Input.GetKeyDown(KeyCode.Space)) {
        // Perform the jump action
        Jump();
    }

    // Check if the "Fire" key (e.g., Ctrl or Mouse
Click) is pressed
    if (Input.GetButtonDown("Fire1")) {
        // Perform the firing action
        Fire();
    }
}
```

In this example, the `Update` method is called each frame, and it checks for specific key presses using the `Input` class. You can similarly handle other input types, such as mouse and touch, using Unity's input system.

Remember that user input handling should be responsive, platform-independent, and adaptable to different input devices to provide the best user experience in your 2D games.

## Section 13.4: Animations and Transitions

Animations play a significant role in bringing life and dynamism to 2D games. They are essential for character movement, interactions, and visual feedback. In this section, we'll explore the principles of creating animations and smooth transitions in 2D game development. ### Key Concepts of Animations 1. **Spritesheet Animation** : One common technique for 2D animations involves creating a spritesheet—a single image that contains multiple frames of an animation. By displaying these frames sequentially, you can create the illusion of movement. 2. **Frame Rate** : The frame rate determines how quickly individual frames are displayed in an animation. A higher frame rate results in smoother animations but may require more resources. Common frame rates are 30 or 60 frames per second (FPS). 3. **Interpolation** : Interpolation techniques, such as linear or eased interpolation, are used to create smooth transitions between animation frames. Easing functions can make animations more realistic by simulating acceleration and deceleration. 4. **Animation States** : In many games, characters or objects have different states (e.g., idle, walking, jumping). Transitions between states should be handled smoothly to avoid abrupt changes. ### Animation Tools and Frameworks

To create animations effectively, you can use various tools and frameworks tailored for 2D game development: 1. **Sprite Animation Software** : Tools like Aseprite, Pyxel Edit, and Adobe Animate allow you to create and edit spritesheets and animations efficiently. 2. **Animation Libraries** : Many game engines and frameworks offer built-in animation systems. For example, Unity's Animator allows you to design complex state machines for character animations. 3. **Tweening Libraries** : Tweening libraries (e.g., DOTween, LeanTween) simplify the interpolation and transition between animation states, making it easier to create smooth transitions. ### Example Animation Code in Unity (C#)

In Unity, you can create animations using the Animator component and C# scripts. Here's a simplified example of animating a 2D character's movement:

```csharp
public class CharacterController : MonoBehaviour {
    private Animator animator;

    private void Start() {
        animator = GetComponent<Animator>();
    }

    private void Update() {
        float horizontalInput =
Input.GetAxis("Horizontal");
        float verticalInput =
Input.GetAxis("Vertical");

        Vector2 moveDirection = new
Vector2(horizontalInput, verticalInput).normalized;

        // Update the Animator parameters for movement
        animator.SetFloat("Speed",
moveDirection.magnitude);

        // Move the character
        transform.Translate(moveDirection * moveSpeed *
Time.deltaTime);
    }
}
```

In this code, the character's movement animation is controlled by updating the "Speed" parameter of the Animator based on user input. The Animator transitions between different

animation states (e.g., walking, idle) based on this parameter.
### Transitioning Between Animations

Smooth transitions between animations can be achieved by defining animation states and transitions in your game engine or framework. For instance, you can set up transitions to smoothly switch from an "idle" state to a "walk" state when the character starts moving.

By mastering animation principles and utilizing the right tools, you can create captivating and visually appealing 2D games with fluid and engaging animations.

## Section 13.5: Debugging and Profiling 2D Graphics

Debugging and profiling are crucial aspects of 2D graphics development that help identify and resolve issues in your game, optimize performance, and ensure a smooth gaming experience. In this section, we'll delve into the techniques and tools for debugging and profiling 2D graphics. ### Debugging Techniques 1. **Console Logging** : One of the simplest debugging techniques is using console logs to print variable values, function calls, or debug messages. This is particularly useful for tracking the flow of your code and identifying issues. 2. **Visual Debugging** : Many game engines and frameworks provide visual debugging tools that allow you to visualize the state of your game objects, such as bounding boxes, collision shapes, and rendering layers. These tools can help you identify issues with object positioning and collision detection. 3. **Error Handling** : Implement proper error handling in your code to catch and handle exceptions gracefully. This prevents crashes and provides users with meaningful error messages, making it easier to diagnose problems. 4. **Breakpoints** : Integrated development environments (IDEs) offer the ability to set breakpoints in your code. When execution reaches a breakpoint, it pauses, allowing you to inspect variable values and the call stack. 5. **Assertions** : Use assertions to validate assumptions in your code. If an assertion fails, it indicates a critical error, and the program may terminate or log the issue for further investigation. ### Profiling for Performance Optimization

Profiling involves analyzing the performance of your game to identify bottlenecks and areas where optimization is needed. Here are some profiling techniques for 2D graphics: 1. **FPS Monitoring** : Keep an eye on the frames per second (FPS) your game achieves. A consistent and high FPS is essential for smooth gameplay. Profiling tools often display FPS alongside other metrics. 2. **CPU and GPU Profiling** : Profiling tools can measure CPU and GPU usage, helping you identify which part of your code consumes the most resources. This is crucial for optimizing performance. 3. **Memory Profiling** : Memory leaks can lead to crashes and poor performance. Profiling tools can help you identify memory leaks by tracking memory allocations and deallocations. 4. **Frame Timing Analysis** : Profiling tools often provide frame timing information, showing how much time is spent on different tasks during each frame. This can reveal areas that need optimization. ### Profiling Tools

Several profiling tools and libraries can assist you in debugging and optimizing 2D graphics: 1. **Unity Profiler** : If you're using Unity, the built-in Profiler is a powerful tool for monitoring CPU and GPU performance, memory usage, and frame timing. It provides a visual representation of these metrics. 2. **Visual Studio Profiler** : If you're using Visual Studio for development, it offers a built-in profiler for .NET applications, including Unity projects. It can help you analyze CPU usage and memory allocation. 3. **RenderDoc** : RenderDoc is a popular open-source graphics debugger and profiler that works with various graphics APIs. It allows you to capture frames, inspect draw calls, and analyze GPU performance. 4. **Intel GPA (Graphics Performance Analyzers)** : This tool is useful for optimizing graphics applications on Intel integrated graphics. It provides insights into GPU performance and offers frame capture and analysis. 5. **Valgrind** : If you're working on Linux, Valgrind is a memory analysis tool that can help you detect memory-related issues and leaks.

Effective debugging and profiling practices are essential for delivering high-quality 2D games. By using these techniques and tools, you can identify and address performance bottlenecks and ensure that your game runs smoothly on a variety of platforms.

# Chapter 14: Graphics Debugging and Optimization Tools

## Section 14.1: GPU Debugging and Profiling Tools

GPU debugging and profiling tools are essential for identifying and resolving graphics-related issues in your applications. These tools provide insights into GPU performance, shader debugging, and frame analysis, helping you optimize your graphics code for better efficiency and visual quality. ### GPU Debugging Tools 1. **NVIDIA Nsight** : Nsight is a comprehensive GPU debugging and profiling tool for NVIDIA GPUs. It allows you to inspect GPU activities, debug shaders, and capture frames for analysis. Nsight supports popular APIs like DirectX, Vulkan, and OpenGL. 2. **AMD Radeon GPU Profiler (RGP)** : RGP is AMD's GPU profiler, designed to analyze the performance of Radeon GPUs. It offers real-time GPU metrics, shader debugging, and frame profiling for DirectX 12 and Vulkan applications. 3. **RenderDoc** : While RenderDoc is primarily known as a graphics debugger, it also includes GPU debugging capabilities. You can use it to capture frames, inspect GPU draw calls, and analyze shader execution. It supports multiple graphics APIs, making it a versatile tool. 4. **Intel GPA (Graphics Performance Analyzers)** : Intel GPA provides GPU debugging and profiling features for Intel integrated graphics. It helps you identify performance bottlenecks and shader issues, making it suitable for optimizing graphics applications on Intel GPUs. 5. **PIX (Performance Investigator for Xbox)** : PIX is Microsoft's GPU debugging and performance analysis tool for Xbox game development. It offers features like GPU captures, shader debugging, and frame analysis specific to Xbox hardware. ### Profiling GPU Performance

Profiling GPU performance is crucial for optimizing graphics applications. These tools help you identify bottlenecks and understand how your GPU resources are utilized: 1. **GPU-Z** : GPU-Z is a lightweight utility that provides real-time monitoring of GPU metrics, such as temperature, clock speeds, and memory usage. While it doesn't offer in-depth profiling, it's useful for quickly checking GPU health. 2. **GPUPerfAPI** : The GPUPerfAPI is a cross-vendor GPU performance library that allows you to collect GPU performance metrics in your application. It supports AMD, NVIDIA, and Intel GPUs and is useful for custom GPU profiling. 3. **NVIDIA PerfHUD** : PerfHUD is a legacy tool from NVIDIA that focuses on performance analysis for DirectX 9 and DirectX 10 applications. While it's older, it can still be valuable for analyzing older graphics projects. 4. **Intel Graphics Performance Analyzers (GPA)** : In addition to debugging, Intel GPA includes GPU performance profiling capabilities. It provides metrics and frame analysis for Intel integrated graphics. 5. **GPU Profilers in Game Engines** : If you're developing games using engines like Unity or Unreal Engine, they often include built-in GPU profilers. These tools integrate seamlessly with your development environment and provide GPU-specific insights.

GPU debugging and profiling tools are indispensable for graphics developers. They help identify performance bottlenecks, optimize shaders, and ensure your graphics-intensive applications run smoothly on a wide range of GPUs. Familiarize yourself with these tools to enhance your graphics development workflow and deliver high-quality visuals in your applications.

## Section 14.2: CPU Profiling and Optimization

While GPU profiling is crucial for graphics programming, it's equally important to optimize CPU performance, as the CPU plays a significant role in managing and preparing data for rendering. In this section, we'll explore CPU profiling tools and techniques to identify and address bottlenecks in your graphics applications. ### CPU Profiling Tools 1. **Visual Studio Profiler** : If you're using Visual Studio for development, it provides a built-in profiler for CPU analysis. You can use it to profile CPU usage, memory allocation, and function-level performance. It's particularly useful for debugging and optimizing C++ code. 2. **Intel VTune Profiler** : Intel's VTune Profiler is a powerful CPU profiling tool that offers deep insights into code performance. It supports various programming languages and can analyze both single-threaded and multi-threaded applications. VTune can help you identify hotspots, threading issues, and memory bottlenecks. 3. **AMD CodeXL** : AMD's CodeXL is a profiling and debugging tool that supports both CPU and GPU profiling. It's especially valuable for AMD CPU analysis, providing metrics, call graphs, and memory usage data. 4. **gprof** : If you're working on Unix-based systems, gprof is a command-line profiler that comes with the GNU Compiler Collection (GCC). It can help you identify performance bottlenecks in your C or C++ code by generating call graphs and flat profiles. 5. **Perf (Linux perf)** : Perf is a performance analysis tool on Linux systems. It offers a wide range of profiling capabilities, including CPU, memory, and instruction-level profiling. Perf can help you analyze system-wide performance and pinpoint CPU bottlenecks. ### Profiling Techniques 1. **Sampling Profiling** : Sampling profilers periodically interrupt your program's execution to capture the call stack. They provide a statistical overview of where your program spends its time. Sampling profilers are lightweight and have minimal impact on program execution. 2. **Instrumentation Profiling** : Instrumentation profilers insert code into your program to collect data on function execution times, memory allocations, and more. While they offer more detailed insights, they can be intrusive and affect program behavior. 3. **Multi-Threading Analysis** : Many CPU profiling tools can analyze multi-threaded applications. Understanding thread interactions and identifying synchronization bottlenecks is crucial for optimizing CPU-bound tasks in graphics programming. 4. **Memory Analysis** : Profiling tools often include memory analysis features. Identifying memory leaks and excessive memory usage is essential for stable and efficient graphics applications. 5. **Function-Level Profiling** : Profilers can help you identify specific functions that consume the most CPU time.

This information is valuable for optimizing critical parts of your code. ### Optimization Strategies

Once you've identified CPU bottlenecks using profiling tools, you can employ several optimization strategies: 1. **Algorithmic Optimization** : Reevaluate your algorithms and data structures. Sometimes, choosing more efficient algorithms or reducing unnecessary computations can lead to significant performance improvements. 2. **Parallelization** : If your application can benefit from parallel processing, consider using multi-threading or GPU compute shaders to offload CPU workloads. 3. **Data-Oriented Design** : Adopt a data-oriented design approach where you organize your data for cache efficiency. This can lead to substantial CPU performance gains. 4. **Reducing Function Calls** : Minimize function calls and inline small, frequently used functions to reduce overhead. 5. **Memory Management** : Optimize memory usage by reducing unnecessary allocations, using object pools, and minimizing memory fragmentation. 6. **Compiler Optimizations** : Explore compiler flags and options for optimization. Modern compilers can perform various optimizations, so make sure to enable them.

CPU profiling and optimization are crucial aspects of graphics programming. By using profiling tools and applying optimization techniques, you can ensure that your graphics applications not only look great but also run efficiently on a wide range of hardware configurations.

## Section 14.3: Graphics Debugging Techniques

Debugging graphics applications can be challenging due to the complexity of modern GPUs and the parallel nature of rendering pipelines. In this section, we will explore various graphics debugging techniques and tools to help you identify and fix issues in your rendering code. ### Debugging Graphics Shaders 1. **Shader Debugging** : Debugging shaders can be tricky because they run on the GPU, and traditional CPU debugging tools may not be applicable. Graphics APIs like OpenGL and Vulkan provide shader debugging extensions and tools. These tools allow you to inspect shader variables, set breakpoints, and step through shader code. 2. **Shader Validation** : Always validate your shader code for syntax errors and logical issues before attempting to run them. Shader compilation errors can be cryptic, so checking for errors at compile time is crucial. 3. **Shader Logging** : Implement shader logging in your application to capture shader compilation and runtime errors. This can help you identify issues more easily during development. ### GPU Profiling 1. **GPU Profilers** : Use GPU profiling tools provided by graphics APIs or third-party applications. These tools capture GPU performance data, such as the time spent on rendering tasks, pipeline stalls, and memory usage. They are essential for identifying GPU bottlenecks. 2. **Frame Capture** : Frame capture tools allow you to capture and inspect rendered frames step by step. They help you analyze the state of the GPU at various points in the rendering process, making it easier to pinpoint rendering issues. ### Render Debugging 1. **Debug Visualizations** : Implement debug visualizations in your application to highlight specific rendering elements, such as bounding boxes, wireframes, or normals. These visualizations can help you verify that objects are positioned and rendered correctly. 2. **Validation Layers** : Graphics APIs like Vulkan provide validation layers that check for common errors in your rendering commands. Enabling these layers during development can catch issues early. ### Resource Tracking 1. **Resource Tracking** : Keep track of GPU resources like textures, buffers, and shaders. Ensure that resources are created, used, and destroyed correctly to prevent resource leaks and memory fragmentation. ### Frame Analysis 1. **Frame Analysis Tools** : Use frame analysis tools to examine the rendering pipeline's behavior for a specific frame. These tools provide insights into the GPU's workload, bottlenecks, and dependencies between rendering stages. ### Code Profiling 1. **Code Profilers** : In addition to GPU profiling, use CPU profiling tools to analyze the CPU-side aspects of your graphics application. These tools can help you identify CPU bottlenecks and optimize code that prepares data for rendering. ### Reproducing Bugs 1. **Reproducible Test Cases** : When you encounter a graphics bug, create a minimal test case that reproduces the issue. Isolating the problem in a smaller codebase makes it easier to debug and fix. 2. **Version Control** : Use version control systems like Git to track changes in your codebase. This allows you to identify when and where issues were introduced and helps in collaboration with team members. 3. **Bisection** : If you're using version control, bisection is a technique where you systematically narrow down the commit that introduced a bug. This can save a lot of debugging time.

Debugging graphics applications is a skill that improves with practice. By using a combination of tools, techniques, and a methodical approach, you can effectively identify and resolve issues in your graphics code, leading to more robust and visually appealing applications.

## Section 14.4: Performance Analysis Tools

Analyzing the performance of your graphics application is crucial for ensuring it runs smoothly and efficiently. In this section, we will explore various performance analysis tools that can help you identify bottlenecks and optimize your rendering code. ### Profiling Tools 1. **CPU Profilers** : CPU profilers are essential for understanding how much time your application spends on different parts of the code. Profilers like perf on Linux or Visual Studio's profiler on Windows can help you identify CPU bottlenecks. 2. **GPU Profilers** : GPU profilers, such as NVIDIA's Nsight or AMD's Radeon GPU Profiler, allow you to capture GPU performance data. They provide insights into GPU bottlenecks, including shader performance, memory usage, and synchronization issues. ### Frame Timing Analysis 1. **Frame Timing Analysis** : Frame timing analysis tools capture the time it takes to render each frame. These tools help you identify spikes or irregularities in frame times, which can indicate rendering issues. Frame timing analysis is particularly crucial for VR and real-time applications. ### RenderDoc 1. **RenderDoc** : RenderDoc is a popular open-source graphics debugger and profiler. It allows you to capture frames, inspect resources, and analyze the rendering pipeline step by step. RenderDoc supports various graphics APIs, including DirectX, OpenGL, and Vulkan.

### GPU Vendor Tools 1. **NVIDIA Nsight** : NVIDIA provides Nsight Graphics and Nsight Compute for profiling and debugging GPU applications. Nsight Graphics supports DirectX, OpenGL, and Vulkan, while Nsight Compute focuses on CUDA and OpenCL. 2. **AMD Radeon GPU Profiler** : AMD offers the Radeon GPU Profiler (RGP), which is a performance analysis tool for AMD GPUs. RGP provides detailed information about GPU execution and memory usage. ### API-Specific Tools 1. **Vulkan SDK** : The Vulkan SDK includes valuable tools for debugging and profiling Vulkan applications. These tools include validation layers, GPU debugging, and frame capture capabilities. 2. **OpenGL Debugging Tools** : If you're working with OpenGL, tools like Apitrace and glslValidator can help you capture frames, inspect OpenGL state, and validate shader code. ### Metrics and Counters 1. **Performance Counters** : Modern GPUs provide performance counters that can be accessed using profiling tools. These counters measure various GPU metrics, such as GPU utilization, memory bandwidth, and cache performance. 2. **GPU-Z and GPU Shark** : GPU-Z and GPU Shark are lightweight tools that provide real-time information about your GPU, including temperature, clock speeds, and GPU load. While not profiling tools, they can be handy for monitoring GPU health during development. ### Tutorials and Documentation 1. **Vendor Documentation** : GPU manufacturers often provide detailed documentation and tutorials on using their profiling and debugging tools. These resources can help you get the most out of the tools available for your specific GPU. 2. **Online Resources** : Online communities and forums, such as the NVIDIA Developer Forums or AMD DevGurus, are excellent places to seek advice and guidance on performance analysis tools and techniques. ### Continuous Profiling 1. **Continuous Profiling** : Consider integrating continuous profiling into your development process. This involves running performance analysis tools regularly to detect and address performance regressions as soon as they occur.

Remember that effective performance analysis requires a combination of tools, techniques, and a deep understanding of your graphics application. Regular profiling and optimization efforts can lead to significant improvements in your application's performance and user experience.

## Section 14.5: Troubleshooting Common Graphics Issues

Graphics programming can be complex, and developers often encounter common issues that can affect the performance and visual quality of their applications. In this section, we'll discuss some of these common graphics issues and how to troubleshoot them effectively. ### 1. **Flickering or Z-Fighting**

Flickering or Z-fighting occurs when two or more objects in a 3D scene occupy nearly the same space, causing them to flicker or appear unstable. This issue is usually due to precision errors in depth calculations. To address it, you can: - Adjust the near and far clip planes to increase depth precision. - Use techniques like "depth bias" to offset depths slightly to avoid Z-fighting. ### 2. **Texture Artifacts or Wrapping**

Texture artifacts may appear when textures are tiled or wrapped incorrectly. To solve this issue: - Ensure textures have power-of-two dimensions or use texture filtering. - Adjust texture addressing modes (e.g., clamp or repeat) to control how textures wrap. ### 3. **Aliasing and Jagged Edges**

Aliasing occurs when diagonal lines or curved edges appear jagged due to low-resolution rendering. To reduce aliasing: - Implement anti-aliasing techniques like multisampling or supersampling. - Use higher-quality texture filtering methods, such as anisotropic filtering. ### 4. **Performance Bottlenecks**

Performance bottlenecks can lead to low frame rates and poor user experiences. To identify and address them: - Use profiling tools to pinpoint CPU and GPU bottlenecks. - Optimize shaders and rendering techniques. - Reduce the complexity of scenes by implementing level-of-detail (LOD) systems. - Implement culling techniques to avoid rendering objects outside the view frustum. ### 5. **Transparency Sorting Issues**

Rendering transparent objects can be challenging, as incorrect sorting can lead to visual artifacts. To address transparency sorting issues: - Use a correct sorting algorithm for transparent objects based on their distance from the camera. - Implement order-independent transparency (OIT) techniques if sorting is not feasible. ### 6. **Shader Compilation Errors**

Shader compilation errors can occur due to syntax errors or unsupported features. To troubleshoot shader issues: - Carefully review shader code for syntax errors and unsupported features. - Check shader compiler error logs for detailed information. - Update shaders to meet the requirements of the graphics API and GPU. ### 7. **Texture Loading Problems**

Texture loading problems can result in missing or corrupted textures. To troubleshoot: - Verify the file format and path of texture files. - Implement error handling in your texture loading code to handle missing or corrupted files gracefully. ### 8. **Memory Leaks**

Memory leaks can lead to performance degradation over time. To detect and resolve memory leaks: - Use memory profiling tools to identify areas of your code that leak memory. - Ensure proper resource cleanup and deallocation. ### 9. **Shader Artifacts**

Shader artifacts may manifest as unexpected visual glitches in rendering. To troubleshoot shader artifacts: - Check shader code for logic errors or incorrect calculations. - Debug shaders by using visualization techniques like rendering intermediate values to textures. ### 10. **Compatibility Issues**

Compatibility issues can arise when targeting different GPUs or platforms. To address compatibility problems: - Test your application on a range of hardware configurations. - Implement feature detection and fallback mechanisms for unsupported features. ### 11. **Driver Updates**

Outdated or buggy graphics drivers can cause issues. Always keep your graphics drivers up to date and be aware of potential driver-related problems.

Troubleshooting common graphics issues requires a combination of debugging techniques, careful code review, and a deep understanding of graphics programming principles. Regular testing and iteration are key to identifying and resolving these issues, ultimately leading to a smoother and more visually appealing graphics application.

# Chapter 15: Graphics Programming Challenges

## Section 15.1: Handling Large Worlds and Terrain

Developing graphics applications often involves the challenge of rendering large and complex virtual worlds. These worlds may encompass vast terrains, cities, or even entire planets. Handling such large-scale environments efficiently is crucial for maintaining real-time rendering performance and providing an immersive user experience. ### The Importance of Efficient Terrain Rendering

One common element in large virtual worlds is terrain. Terrain rendering involves generating and rendering the landscape, which can consist of mountains, valleys, forests, and more. Rendering large terrains efficiently is essential for open-world games, flight simulators, and virtual exploration experiences. #### Terrain Data Representation

To render large terrains, you need an efficient representation of the terrain data. One widely used approach is heightmap-based terrain representation. A heightmap is a 2D grid where each pixel represents the height (elevation) of a point on the terrain. Heightmaps are easy to understand and work with, making them a popular choice.

```
// Example heightmap data
float heightmap[MAP_SIZE][MAP_SIZE];
```

*Level of Detail (LOD) Techniques*

Level of Detail (LOD) techniques are crucial for efficient terrain rendering. LOD involves adjusting the level of detail in the terrain based on the viewer's distance. When the viewer is far away, rendering every detail of the terrain is unnecessary and wasteful. LOD techniques reduce the detail level as the viewer moves farther from the terrain, resulting in substantial performance improvements. #### Terrain Paging and Culling

Paging and culling are techniques used to load and render only the portions of the terrain that are visible to the viewer. This involves dividing the terrain into smaller chunks or pages and dynamically loading and unloading them as the viewer moves. Additionally, frustum culling is employed to determine which chunks are within the camera's view frustum, further reducing rendering overhead. ### Optimizing Large-World Rendering

In addition to terrain rendering, large-world environments often contain various objects, vegetation, and dynamic elements. Optimizing the rendering of these elements is equally important. #### Occlusion Culling

Occlusion culling is a technique used to avoid rendering objects that are entirely or partially occluded by other objects. This reduces unnecessary rendering work and improves performance. Techniques like occlusion queries or visibility buffers can be employed to implement occlusion culling effectively. #### Dynamic Level of Detail (DLOD)

For objects and elements within the large world that are not part of the terrain, dynamic level of detail (DLOD) techniques can be used. Similar to terrain LOD, DLOD adjusts the detail level of objects based on their distance from the viewer. This ensures that only the necessary details are rendered for each object, saving GPU resources. ### Challenges and Trade-Offs

Efficiently rendering large worlds and terrains involves several trade-offs. Increasing rendering efficiency may lead to compromises in visual fidelity. Balancing performance and visual quality is a continuous challenge for graphics programmers working on large-scale environments. ### Conclusion

Handling large worlds and terrains in graphics programming is a complex task that requires a combination of data representation, LOD techniques, culling methods, and optimization strategies. Successfully addressing these challenges is crucial for delivering immersive and high-performance graphics experiences in open-world games, simulations, and virtual environments.

## Section 15.2: Real-Time Fluid Simulation

Simulating realistic fluids, such as water, smoke, or fire, is a challenging and computationally intensive task in graphics programming. Real-time fluid simulation is essential for creating visually engaging and interactive environments, particularly in video games and simulations. In this section, we'll explore some key concepts and techniques used in real-time fluid simulation. ### Fluid Dynamics Basics

Fluid simulation is based on the principles of fluid dynamics, a branch of physics that studies the behavior of fluids (liquids and gases). Key components of fluid simulation include modeling fluid properties like density, velocity, and pressure. The Navier-Stokes equations are often used as the foundation for simulating fluid behavior.

$$\partial u/\partial t + u \cdot \nabla u = -\nabla p + v\nabla^2 u + f$$

Here, u represents velocity, p is pressure, v is viscosity, and f represents external forces like gravity. Solving these equations in real-time to simulate fluid behavior is a computationally intensive process. ### Grid-Based Fluid Simulation

One common approach to real-time fluid simulation is grid-based methods. These methods discretize the fluid domain into a grid of cells. Each cell stores information about fluid properties, such as velocity and density. Several techniques exist, including the Marker-and-Cell (MAC) method and the Fluid Implicit

Particle (FLIP) method, which simulate fluid behavior using grids.

```
// Grid-based fluid simulation data structures
struct GridCell {
    Vector3 velocity;
    float density;
};
```

```
// Grid representing the fluid domain
GridCell fluidGrid[GRID_SIZE][GRID_SIZE][GRID_SIZE];
```

Grid-based simulations allow for efficient computation of fluid dynamics by updating properties in discrete cells. However, they may struggle with capturing small-scale details and tend to be less accurate than particle-based methods for turbulent flows.

### Particle-Based Fluid Simulation

Particle-based fluid simulation, on the other hand, models fluids using individual particles that interact with each other based on physical principles. This approach is more accurate for capturing complex fluid behavior, such as splashing, swirling, and turbulence.

```
// Particle-based fluid simulation data structures
struct FluidParticle {
    Vector3 position;
    Vector3 velocity;
};
```

```
std::vector<FluidParticle> fluidParticles;
```

Particle-based methods, like Smoothed Particle Hydrodynamics (SPH) and Position-Based Fluids (PBF), simulate fluid behavior by applying forces between neighboring particles, including pressure, viscosity, and surface tension forces.

### Challenges and Optimization

Real-time fluid simulation faces several challenges, including computational complexity, stability, and scalability. Optimizations like parallel computing on GPUs, adaptive time-stepping, and spatial data structures (e.g., spatial hashing) are essential for achieving real-time performance. ### Conclusion

Real-time fluid simulation is a complex and fascinating area of graphics programming. It plays a crucial role in creating visually stunning and interactive environments in games and simulations. Balancing realism and computational efficiency remains a constant challenge, and ongoing research in this field continues to push the boundaries of what's possible in real-time fluid dynamics.

## Section 15.3: Cloth and Cloth Simulation

Cloth simulation is a fundamental component of many graphics applications, from video games to animation and virtual fashion design. It involves simulating the behavior of flexible materials like cloth, leather, or rubber. In this section, we'll delve into the concepts and techniques behind cloth simulation in graphics programming. ### Mass-Spring Systems

Cloth simulation is often based on the concept of mass-spring systems. In this approach, the cloth is divided into a grid of points connected by springs. Each point (also called a mass) has properties like position, velocity, and mass. The springs model the internal forces within the cloth, such as stretching and bending.

```
struct Mass {
    Vector3 position;
    Vector3 velocity;
    float mass;
};

struct Spring {
    Mass* point1;
    Mass* point2;
    float restLength;
    float stiffness;
};
```

The forces acting on each mass point include gravity, damping, and the spring forces. The cloth's behavior emerges from the interactions of these elements. ### Numerical Integration

To simulate cloth motion, numerical integration methods like the Verlet integration or the explicit Euler method are commonly used. These methods update the positions and velocities of mass points over time based on the forces acting on them.

```
// Verlet integration
void VerletIntegration(Mass* mass) {
    Vector3 newPosition = 2 * mass->position - mass-
>prevPosition + mass->acceleration * deltaTime *
deltaTime;
    mass->prevPosition = mass->position;
    mass->position = newPosition;
}
```

```
// Explicit Euler integration
void EulerIntegration(Mass* mass) {
    mass->velocity += mass->acceleration * deltaTime;
    mass->position += mass->velocity * deltaTime;
}
```

These integration methods help approximate the cloth's dynamic behavior while ensuring stability. ### Cloth Constraints

Cloth simulation also involves constraints to maintain the cloth's shape and prevent unrealistic stretching and bending. Constraints like distance constraints for springs and angle constraints for bending help the cloth maintain its structural integrity.

```
// Distance constraint between two mass points
void ApplyDistanceConstraint(Spring* spring) {
    Vector3 delta = spring->point2->position - spring-
>point1->position;
    float currentDistance = length(delta);
    Vector3 correction = delta * (1 - spring-
>restLength / currentDistance) * 0.5f;
    spring->point1->position += correction;
```

```
    spring->point2->position -= correction;
}
```

Cloth Simulation Challenges

Cloth simulation can be computationally expensive, especially when dealing with a large number of mass points and springs. Optimizations like spatial partitioning and parallelization can be employed to achieve real-time performance. Additionally, handling cloth collisions with other objects in the scene is another challenge in cloth simulation. ### Conclusion

Cloth simulation is a crucial element of graphics programming, enabling the realistic depiction of various materials in virtual environments. Understanding mass-spring systems, numerical integration, and constraint handling is essential for implementing cloth simulations that meet the demands of modern graphics applications. As hardware capabilities continue to advance, we can expect even more realistic and interactive cloth simulations in the future.

## Section 15.4: Implementing AI and Pathfinding in Games

Artificial Intelligence (AI) and pathfinding are critical components of modern video games that contribute to creating lifelike and engaging gameplay experiences. In this section, we'll explore the role of AI in games and delve into various pathfinding algorithms commonly used to make game characters navigate complex environments. ### Role of AI in Games

AI in games refers to the algorithms and techniques used to simulate intelligent behavior in non-player characters (NPCs) or entities within the game world. Game AI is responsible for various aspects of gameplay, including enemy behavior, decision-making, and pathfinding. It aims to make NPCs seem intelligent and responsive to the player's actions. #### Decision-Making

Decision-making is a fundamental aspect of game AI. NPCs must decide how to react to the player's actions or other in-game events. Decision trees, behavior trees, finite state machines (FSMs), and rule-based systems are commonly used approaches to model NPC decision-making. #### Pathfinding

Pathfinding involves finding the optimal or near-optimal path from one point to another in a game environment. This is crucial for NPCs to navigate terrain, avoid obstacles, and reach their goals. Several pathfinding algorithms are employed to achieve this. ### Pathfinding Algorithms #### A* Algorithm

The A* algorithm is one of the most popular and versatile pathfinding algorithms used in games. It combines the strengths of Dijkstra's algorithm and heuristic approaches to efficiently find the shortest path. A* considers both the cost of the path traveled so far and an estimate of the cost to reach the destination, making it highly efficient for grid-based and node-based pathfinding.

```
# Pseudocode for A* algorithm
open_set = priority_queue()
open_set.add(start_node)

while not open_set.empty():
    current_node = open_set.pop()

    if current_node == goal_node:
        reconstruct_path()
        break

    for neighbor in current_node.neighbors:
        tentative_g_score = current_node.g_score +
distance(current_node, neighbor)
        if tentative_g_score < neighbor.g_score:
            neighbor.came_from = current_node
            neighbor.g_score = tentative_g_score
            neighbor.f_score = neighbor.g_score +
heuristic(neighbor, goal_node)
            if neighbor not in open_set:
                open_set.add(neighbor)
```

## Dijkstra's Algorithm

Dijkstra's algorithm, although less commonly used in games due to its computational cost, is an excellent choice for finding the shortest path in weighted graphs where all edge weights are non-negative. It guarantees the shortest path but can be slower for large graphs.

```
# Pseudocode for Dijkstra's algorithm
while unvisited_nodes:
    current_node = node with the lowest tentative
distance
    unvisited_nodes.remove(current_node)

    for neighbor in current_node.neighbors:
        tentative_distance = current_node.distance +
distance(current_node, neighbor)
        if tentative_distance < neighbor.distance:
            neighbor.distance = tentative_distance
            neighbor.previous = current_node
```

## Other Algorithms

Various other pathfinding algorithms, such as the Breadth-First Search (BFS), Depth-First Search (DFS), and the Jump Point Search (JPS), are used depending on the specific requirements of the game and the nature of the game world. ### Conclusion

AI and pathfinding are integral parts of game development, enhancing player experiences by creating dynamic and intelligent NPCs and enabling them to navigate complex game environments. Understanding the principles of AI and various pathfinding algorithms is crucial for game developers aiming to create immersive and challenging gameplay. As technology continues to advance, AI in games will become even more sophisticated, providing players with increasingly realistic and interactive virtual worlds.

## Section 15.5: Networked Multiplayer Graphics

Networked multiplayer gaming has become an integral part of the gaming industry, enabling players from around the world to connect and compete or cooperate in online game worlds. In this section, we'll explore the challenges and considerations related to networked multiplayer graphics and the techniques used to create seamless and immersive multiplayer experiences. ### The Importance of Networked Multiplayer Graphics

Networked multiplayer games require synchronization of game state, including graphics, among multiple players connected to a server. Achieving smooth and consistent gameplay experiences in networked multiplayer games is crucial for player engagement and enjoyment. Networked multiplayer graphics encompass several key aspects: #### Latency and Lag

Reducing latency and minimizing lag is paramount in networked multiplayer graphics. High latency or lag can result in delayed actions, which can significantly impact the gameplay experience. Techniques like client-side prediction and lag compensation are employed to mitigate these issues. #### Bandwidth and Data Transmission

Transmitting graphics data efficiently over the network is essential. Graphics assets, such as textures and models, must be loaded and synchronized among players without overwhelming limited bandwidth. Data compression, streaming, and delta updates are some of the strategies used. #### Game State Synchronization

Maintaining consistent game state across all connected clients is a complex task. Game state includes the positions, animations, and interactions of all players and objects in the game world. Techniques like lockstep synchronization and authoritative server architecture help achieve this. ### Techniques for Networked Multiplayer Graphics #### Client-Side Prediction

Client-side prediction involves allowing the local player's client to make immediate game state updates based on user input without waiting for confirmation from the server. This can lead to smoother gameplay by reducing perceived latency. However, server reconciliation is necessary to correct any discrepancies.

#### Lag Compensation

Lag compensation aims to provide a fair and consistent experience for players with varying network latencies. It involves rewinding and replaying game state to compensate for the time it takes for player actions to reach the server.

#### Delta Compression

Delta compression involves transmitting only the changes or differences in game state between frames instead of sending the entire state each time. This reduces bandwidth usage and speeds up data transmission.

#### Authoritative Server

In an authoritative server architecture, the server holds the ultimate authority over the game state. Clients send input commands to the server, which processes them and broadcasts the resulting game state to all clients. This ensures fairness and security but can introduce some latency.

#### Peer-to-Peer (P2P) Networking

Some multiplayer games use P2P networking, where players communicate directly with each other rather than through a central server. P2P can reduce server load but introduces challenges in ensuring synchronization and security.

### Conclusion

Networked multiplayer graphics represent a significant technological achievement in the gaming industry. They enable players to connect and enjoy games with friends and strangers worldwide. Developing networked multiplayer graphics systems involves addressing challenges related to latency, bandwidth, and game state synchronization. As technology advances, multiplayer experiences will continue to evolve, providing players with even more immersive and seamless gaming adventures.

# Chapter 16: Graphics in Virtual Reality (VR)

## Section 16.1: Introduction to VR Graphics

Virtual Reality (VR) has rapidly emerged as an exciting frontier in the world of graphics and interactive experiences. VR technology immerses users in a simulated environment, enabling them to interact with the digital world in a more natural and engaging way. In this section, we'll provide an introduction to VR graphics, exploring the key concepts, hardware, and rendering techniques that make VR experiences possible. ### Understanding Virtual Reality

Virtual Reality refers to a computer-generated environment that simulates a physical presence in a real or imagined world. It typically involves the use of specialized hardware, including VR headsets, motion controllers, and tracking systems, to provide users with a sense of immersion and presence within the virtual environment. ### VR Hardware Components #### 1. VR Headsets

VR headsets are the primary interface between the user and the virtual world. They feature high-resolution displays that are positioned close to the eyes, creating a stereoscopic 3D effect. Some popular VR headsets include the Oculus Rift, HTC Vive, and PlayStation VR. #### 2. Motion Controllers

Motion controllers allow users to interact with the virtual world using their hands. These controllers are tracked in real-time, enabling precise hand and gesture recognition. They enhance the sense of immersion by providing tactile feedback. #### 3. Tracking Systems

VR tracking systems use various sensors, such as cameras and infrared sensors, to track the position and orientation of the user's head and controllers. This information is used to update the user's view in real-time, ensuring a seamless and responsive experience. ### VR Rendering Challenges

Rendering for VR introduces several unique challenges: #### 1. High Frame Rates

VR demands extremely high frame rates (often 90 frames per second or more) to prevent motion sickness and maintain immersion. Achieving consistent high frame rates requires optimized rendering techniques. #### 2. Low Latency

VR systems require minimal latency between user actions and corresponding changes in the virtual environment. Even slight delays can lead to discomfort and disorientation. #### 3. Stereo Rendering

VR requires rendering two distinct views (one for each eye) to create a 3D effect. This requires careful synchronization and optimization of the rendering pipeline. #### 4. Comfort and Realism

Balancing visual realism with user comfort is essential. Graphics should be convincing without causing discomfort or motion sickness. ### VR Rendering Techniques #### 1. Asynchronous Timewarp (ATW)

ATW is a technique used to reduce perceived latency. It predicts the user's head movement and adjusts the rendered frames accordingly, even if the GPU is not yet finished rendering. #### 2. Foveated Rendering

Foveated rendering optimizes rendering resources by focusing high-quality rendering on the user's gaze point while reducing detail in peripheral areas. This reduces GPU workload without sacrificing perceived quality. #### 3. Stereoscopic Rendering

Stereoscopic rendering involves rendering two slightly different images, one for each eye, to create a 3D effect. This is essential for depth perception in VR. ### Conclusion

VR graphics represent a thrilling frontier in graphics programming, offering immersive experiences that blur the lines between the digital and physical worlds. Understanding VR hardware and addressing the unique rendering challenges are crucial for creating compelling VR applications and games. As VR technology continues to advance, we can expect even more realistic and immersive experiences in the future.

## Section 16.2: VR Headsets and Tracking

Virtual Reality (VR) headsets and tracking systems are at the core of the VR experience. In this section, we will delve deeper into the technology behind VR headsets and tracking solutions, exploring how they work and their significance in creating immersive VR environments. ### VR Headsets

VR headsets are the most recognizable component of a VR setup. They come in various shapes and sizes, but they all share common features and functionalities. Here are some key aspects of VR headsets: #### 1. Display Technology

VR headsets incorporate high-resolution displays positioned close to the user's eyes. These displays are typically OLED or LCD screens with fast refresh rates to minimize motion blur. The proximity of the displays creates a stereoscopic effect, enhancing depth perception. #### 2. Optics

Optical lenses are used to focus the images displayed on the screens. These lenses are designed to reduce distortion and minimize the "screen door effect," where the user perceives the individual pixels on the display. #### 3. Field of View (FoV)

The field of view is the extent of the virtual world that a user can see through the headset. A wider FoV contributes to a more immersive experience. Achieving a wide FoV while maintaining optical quality is a design challenge for VR headset manufacturers. #### 4. Tracking Sensors

VR headsets are equipped with sensors that track the orientation and movement of the user's head. These sensors are essential for updating the view in real-time, ensuring that the user's perspective matches their head movements. #### 5. Audio

Many VR headsets also feature integrated audio solutions, such as headphones or built-in speakers. Spatial audio is often used to enhance immersion, allowing users to perceive sound from different directions. #### 6. Comfort and Ergonomics

Comfort is crucial for prolonged VR sessions. Headsets are designed with adjustable straps, padding, and weight distribution to minimize discomfort and fatigue. ### Tracking Systems #### 1. Inside-Out Tracking

Inside-out tracking, used by headsets like the Oculus Quest, relies on sensors and cameras embedded in the headset itself. These sensors track the position of the headset relative to the environment, enabling room-scale VR experiences without external sensors. #### 2. Outside-In Tracking

Outside-in tracking, employed by systems like the HTC Vive, uses external sensors or cameras placed in the room. These sensors track the position of the headset and controllers by detecting infrared or visual markers on the devices. #### 3. Lighthouse Tracking

Lighthouse tracking, developed by Valve, uses laser-based tracking stations called "Lighthouses." These stations emit laser beams that are picked up by sensors on the headset and controllers, allowing for precise tracking in a room. ### Combining Headsets and Tracking

The combination of high-quality VR headsets and accurate tracking systems is crucial for delivering a seamless and immersive VR experience. Users can explore virtual environments, interact with objects, and engage in gaming or training scenarios with a high degree of realism.

Developers working on VR applications must consider the capabilities and limitations of both headsets and tracking systems when creating content. Additionally, advancements in VR technology continue to push the boundaries of what is possible in terms of immersion and presence, making VR an exciting and dynamic field within graphics programming.

## Section 16.3: VR Rendering Techniques

Virtual Reality (VR) rendering is a specialized area of graphics programming aimed at creating immersive experiences for users wearing VR headsets. In this section, we'll explore some of the key rendering techniques used in VR to achieve smooth and comfortable visuals. ### VR-Specific Challenges

VR presents unique challenges due to its requirement for high frame rates and low-latency rendering to avoid motion sickness. When designing VR applications, developers need to consider the following challenges: #### 1. High Frame Rates

Traditional games may target 30 or 60 frames per second (FPS), but VR demands much higher frame rates, typically 90 FPS or higher. Maintaining a consistent frame rate is crucial to prevent motion sickness. #### 2. Stereoscopic Rendering

VR headsets use stereoscopic displays to create depth perception. This means rendering two slightly different views, one for each eye, to create a 3D effect. The rendering pipeline must handle this efficiently. #### 3. Low Latency

Any delay between a user's head movement and the corresponding change in the VR scene can lead to discomfort. Reducing rendering and input latency is a priority in VR development. #### 4. Optimized Graphics

VR applications need to be optimized for performance. Techniques like level-of-detail (LOD) rendering and efficient culling are crucial to maintain high frame rates. ### VR Rendering Techniques #### 1. Asynchronous Time Warp (ATW)

ATW is a technology used in some VR systems to reduce latency. It predicts the user's head movement and adjusts the rendered frames accordingly, compensating for any delays in the rendering pipeline. #### 2. Foveated Rendering

Foveated rendering takes advantage of the fact that the human eye is most sensitive to detail at the center of vision (the fovea).

By rendering the highest quality graphics only in the user's central field of view and reducing quality in peripheral areas, foveated rendering can significantly reduce rendering workload.

#### 3. Single-Pass Stereo Rendering

To efficiently render separate views for each eye, VR applications often use single-pass stereo rendering techniques provided by graphics APIs like Vulkan and DirectX 12. This reduces CPU and GPU overhead.

#### 4. Asynchronous Spacewarp (ASW)

ASW, used in some VR systems, helps maintain smooth visuals even when the frame rate drops below the target. It uses interpolation to generate intermediate frames, creating the illusion of smooth motion.

#### 5. Multiview Rendering

Multiview rendering, supported by some GPUs and APIs, allows rendering both left and right eye views simultaneously using a single set of draw calls, reducing the rendering workload.

### VR Anti-Aliasing

Anti-aliasing techniques are essential in VR to reduce jaggies and improve image quality. Some VR-specific anti-aliasing methods include:

#### 1. Multisample Anti-Aliasing (MSAA)

MSAA is a common anti-aliasing technique that works well in VR. It smooths jagged edges and enhances image quality.

#### 2. Fast Approximate Anti-Aliasing (FXAA)

FXAA is a post-process anti-aliasing technique that is lightweight and suitable for VR applications where performance is crucial.

#### 3. Super Sampling

Super sampling involves rendering the scene at a higher resolution than the headset's display and downscaling it. This reduces aliasing artifacts and improves image clarity.

### Conclusion

VR rendering is a challenging but exciting field of graphics programming. Developers need to employ various techniques to ensure smooth, low-latency, and visually pleasing experiences for VR users. As VR technology continues to evolve, so too will the rendering techniques and optimizations used to create immersive VR worlds.

## Section 16.4: Interaction and Controllers in VR

Virtual Reality (VR) experiences are not only about immersive visuals but also about user interaction within the virtual environment. To achieve this, VR systems incorporate controllers that enable users to interact with the virtual world. In this section, we'll delve into the essential aspects of VR interaction and controllers. ### VR Controllers

VR controllers are handheld devices designed to mimic users' hand movements and gestures within the virtual environment. These controllers are equipped with various sensors, buttons, and triggers to provide a rich and intuitive interaction experience. #### Tracking Technology

Most VR controllers use tracking technology to determine their position and orientation in 3D space accurately. This tracking can be achieved through methods like: - **Inside-Out Tracking:** Some VR systems have cameras or sensors built into the headset to track controller movement. This approach is more user-friendly as it doesn't require external sensors. - **Outside-In Tracking:** External sensors or cameras placed in the physical environment track the controllers' movements. This method can provide highly accurate tracking but requires additional setup. ### Input Mapping

Mapping physical button presses, gestures, and movements to in-game actions is known as input mapping. VR developers must design intuitive and responsive input mappings to ensure a seamless user experience. #### Gesture Recognition

Many VR controllers are equipped with sensors that can recognize hand gestures. This enables users to perform actions like grabbing objects, pointing, or making thumbs-up gestures within the virtual world. ### Haptic Feedback

Haptic feedback is crucial for enhancing the sense of presence in VR. It provides tactile feedback to users when they interact with virtual objects or surfaces. VR controllers use various mechanisms to deliver haptic feedback, such as vibration motors or more advanced haptic feedback systems that simulate different sensations.

### Interaction Techniques

Developers have created a variety of interaction techniques to enable users to interact with virtual objects realistically. Some common techniques include:

#### 1. Grabbing and Throwing

Users can pick up virtual objects by physically grabbing them with the controllers and release them to throw or drop them.

#### 2. Pointing and Selecting

Pointing at objects in VR and using a controller button to select or interact with them is a straightforward and intuitive interaction technique.

#### 3. Virtual Tools

VR applications often provide virtual tools that users can access from their controllers. These tools may include drawing brushes, weapons, or other specialized objects.

#### 4. Teleportation

To navigate large virtual environments, teleportation is a popular technique. Users point at a location and teleport there instantly, reducing motion sickness.

### Development Platforms

Developers have access to development platforms and software development kits (SDKs) provided by VR hardware manufacturers. For example, Oculus provides the Oculus SDK for its VR headsets, and SteamVR is a platform for multiple VR hardware manufacturers.

### Challenges

Creating effective VR interactions and controllers comes with its own set of challenges, including: - Ensuring precise tracking and low latency to prevent motion sickness. - Designing user interfaces that are easy to understand and use in a 3D space. - Balancing the level of haptic feedback to enhance immersion without becoming uncomfortable. - Optimizing interactions for different VR hardware platforms.

In conclusion, VR controllers and interactions are vital components of creating immersive and engaging VR experiences. Developers must carefully design and implement these aspects to make VR applications intuitive and enjoyable for users. As VR technology continues to advance, the possibilities for more natural and immersive interactions will only grow.

## Section 16.5: Challenges and Considerations in VR Graphics

Virtual Reality (VR) graphics present a unique set of challenges and considerations that developers must address to create immersive and comfortable experiences. In this section, we'll explore some of the key challenges and important factors to consider when developing VR graphics. ### 1. Frame Rate and Performance

Maintaining a high and consistent frame rate is crucial in VR to prevent motion sickness and provide a comfortable experience. VR headsets typically target frame rates of 90 Hz or higher to ensure smooth visuals. Developers must optimize their VR applications to meet these demanding performance requirements, which may include reducing polygon counts, optimizing shaders, and implementing efficient rendering techniques. ### 2. Field of View (FoV)

VR headsets offer a limited field of view compared to the human eye's natural vision. Developers need to adapt their content to fit within this restricted FoV while ensuring that essential information and interactions are not lost outside the visible area. Proper FoV management can help users stay immersed and reduce discomfort. ### 3. Resolution and Pixel Density

Achieving high-resolution graphics is essential for VR to create sharp and realistic visuals. However, rendering at such high resolutions can be taxing on hardware. Developers should strike a balance between resolution and performance, utilizing techniques like dynamic resolution scaling to maintain a stable frame rate. ### 4. Stereoscopic Rendering

VR relies on stereoscopic rendering to create a 3D effect. This involves rendering slightly different images for each eye to simulate depth perception. Developers must ensure that stereoscopic rendering is accurate and properly aligned to prevent visual discomfort and strain. ### 5. Latency

Minimizing latency, the delay between user input and the corresponding visual feedback, is crucial for VR. High latency can lead to motion sickness and disconnect users from the virtual world. Optimizing input and rendering pipelines to reduce latency is a top priority for VR development. ### 6. User Interface (UI) Design

Designing UI elements for VR is different from traditional 2D interfaces. UI components must be readable, interactive, and integrated seamlessly into the 3D environment. Oversized buttons, intuitive controls, and thoughtful placement of UI elements are essential for user comfort and usability. ### 7. Comfort Modes

VR experiences should provide comfort options to accommodate users with varying levels of sensitivity to motion sickness. This includes features like snap turning, teleportation for movement, and adjustable comfort settings. ### 8. Testing and User Feedback

Testing VR applications with real users is essential to identify comfort issues and gather feedback. Conducting playtesting and user studies can help developers refine their applications to make them more comfortable and enjoyable. ### 9. Accessibility

Considerations for accessibility in VR are crucial. Developers should provide options for users with disabilities, such as alternative control schemes, audio cues, and text-to-speech support. ### 10. Content Guidelines

Many VR platforms have content guidelines that developers must adhere to. These guidelines often include recommendations for comfort and safety to ensure that VR experiences are enjoyable for a wide range of users.

In conclusion, developing VR graphics requires careful consideration of factors like performance, comfort, and user experience. By addressing these challenges and adhering to best practices, developers can create VR applications that are visually stunning, comfortable to use, and accessible to a broad audience. As VR technology continues to advance, these considerations will remain central to creating compelling and immersive virtual experiences.

# Chapter 17: Graphics in Augmented Reality (AR)

## Section 17.1: Understanding Augmented Reality

Augmented Reality (AR) is a technology that overlays digital information, such as 3D models, text, or animations, onto the real world. Unlike Virtual Reality (VR), which immerses users in a completely virtual environment, AR enhances the real-world environment by adding computer-generated elements. In this section, we will explore the fundamentals of Augmented Reality, its applications, and the key concepts that underpin AR development. ### What is Augmented Reality?

Augmented Reality blends digital content with the physical world, allowing users to interact with both simultaneously. AR applications use various technologies, such as cameras, sensors, and display devices, to recognize and track real-world objects or locations and superimpose computer-generated elements onto them. This integration of virtual and real-world elements creates a mixed reality experience. ### Key Components of Augmented Reality: 1. **Sensors:** AR devices are equipped with sensors like cameras, accelerometers, and gyroscopes to perceive the physical world. These sensors provide data used for tracking and mapping the environment. 2. **Recognition and Tracking:** AR applications use computer vision algorithms to recognize and track objects or markers in the real world. This enables accurate placement of virtual objects within the user's view. 3. **Display Devices:** AR content is typically displayed through devices like smartphones, tablets, smart glasses, or headsets. These devices provide the user's view of the real world and overlay digital elements onto it. 4. **User Interaction:** AR allows users to interact with virtual objects using touch, voice commands, gestures, or even gaze tracking, depending on the AR platform and device. ### Applications of Augmented Reality:

AR has a wide range of applications across various industries, including: - **Gaming:** AR games like Pokémon GO and ARKit/ARCore-based mobile games have gained immense popularity. - **Education:** AR can enhance learning experiences by providing interactive educational content. - **Retail:** AR is used for virtual try-ons, product visualization, and enhancing in-store experiences. - **Navigation:** AR navigation apps provide real-time information overlaid on the user's view to aid in directions. - **Healthcare:** AR is used for medical training, surgical planning, and visualizing patient data in 3D. - **Manufacturing:** AR assists in assembly, maintenance, and quality control processes. ### Development Platforms for Augmented Reality:

Several platforms and SDKs (Software Development Kits) are available for AR development: - **ARKit and ARCore:** These platforms provide AR capabilities for iOS and Android devices, making AR development accessible to mobile app developers. - **Unity3D:** A popular game engine with AR support, allowing developers to create cross-platform AR applications. - **Vuforia:** An AR development platform that specializes in object recognition and tracking. - **HoloLens:** Microsoft's HoloLens devices and Windows Mixed Reality provide AR development opportunities for PC and headset-based applications.

In summary, Augmented Reality is a transformative technology that merges the digital and physical worlds, offering exciting opportunities for developers to create engaging and immersive experiences across a wide range of industries. Understanding the fundamentals of AR and its components is essential for those looking to explore this innovative field further.

## Section 17.2: AR Displays and Sensors

Augmented Reality (AR) experiences heavily rely on AR displays and sensors to bridge the gap between the digital and physical worlds. These components enable users to see and interact with virtual elements superimposed on their real-world surroundings. In this section, we will delve into AR displays and sensors, understanding how they work and their role in creating immersive AR experiences. ### AR Displays

AR displays are the primary interface through which users perceive augmented content. There are several types of AR displays, each with its own characteristics: 1. **Smartphones and Tablets:** Most people have experienced AR through their smartphones or tablets. These devices use their built-in screens and cameras to display the real world while overlaying digital content. Apps like Pokémon GO and Snapchat filters are popular examples of smartphone-based AR. 2. **Smart Glasses:** Smart glasses, like Google Glass and Microsoft HoloLens, are designed specifically for AR. They provide a see-through display, allowing users to view both the real world and digital information simultaneously. These devices often incorporate sensors for tracking and interaction, creating immersive experiences. 3. **Head-Mounted Displays (HMDs):** AR HMDs, such as those used in VR, can also support AR experiences. These devices offer high-quality displays and precise tracking. When equipped with passthrough cameras, they enable AR applications without obscuring the user's vision. 4. **HUDs (Heads-Up Displays):** HUDs are commonly used in vehicles and aircraft to provide essential information to the user without distraction. While not as immersive as other AR displays, they offer a practical way to overlay data onto the real world. ### AR Sensors

AR sensors are crucial for understanding the user's environment and enabling interactions with virtual objects. Here are some key AR sensors and their functions: 1. **Cameras:** Cameras are the primary visual sensors in AR devices. They capture images or video of the user's surroundings, which are then analyzed for object recognition, tracking, and mapping. Depth-sensing cameras, like the ones in the iPhone X, provide additional data for more accurate AR. 2. **Accelerometers and Gyroscopes:** These sensors measure the device's motion and orientation. They are essential for detecting changes in position and orientation, enabling accurate tracking and stability of virtual objects. 3. **Magnetometers:** Magnetometers, or compass sensors, determine the device's orientation with respect to Earth's magnetic field. This helps in calibrating the device's orientation and improving tracking accuracy. 4. **GPS (Global Positioning System):** While primarily used for location-based services, GPS can enhance AR experiences by providing the user's global position. Combining GPS with visual data allows for geolocation-based AR applications. 5. **Lidar and ToF (Time of Flight) Sensors:** These sensors emit laser or infrared light pulses and measure the time it takes for them to bounce back. This data can create depth maps of the environment, aiding in object recognition and mapping. ### Interaction with AR Displays

In AR, interaction is a crucial aspect of the user experience. Users need intuitive ways to manipulate and engage with virtual elements. Interaction methods include: - **Touch:** On smartphone-based AR, users can interact with virtual objects through touch gestures on the device's screen. - **Voice Commands:** Some AR devices support voice recognition, allowing users to control and interact with virtual elements using voice commands. - **Gesture Recognition:** AR glasses and HMDs often incorporate gesture recognition technology. Users can perform hand gestures to interact with virtual objects or navigate AR menus. - **Controllers:** In some AR applications, handheld controllers are used to provide precise interaction, similar to VR controllers.

In conclusion, AR displays and sensors are the foundation of Augmented Reality experiences. These components enable users to see, interact with, and immerse themselves in digital content overlaid onto their real-world environment. As AR technology continues to advance, we can expect even more innovative displays and sensors, leading to increasingly immersive and interactive AR applications.

## Section 17.3: Marker-Based and Markerless AR

Augmented Reality (AR) applications can be categorized into two main types based on how they recognize and track the user's environment: marker-based and markerless AR. In this section, we'll explore the differences, advantages, and use cases of these two approaches. ### Marker-Based AR

**Marker-based AR** relies on predefined visual markers, usually 2D images or patterns, that the AR system can recognize and track in real time. When the camera captures one of these markers, the AR application can overlay digital content precisely on top of it. Here's how marker-based AR works: 1. **Marker Detection:** The AR software analyzes the camera feed to identify markers within the field of view. This is often done using computer vision techniques like feature detection and image recognition. 2. **Tracking:** Once detected, the AR system continuously tracks the marker's position and orientation as the camera moves. This tracking information is used to position virtual objects in the real world accurately.

**Advantages of Marker-Based AR:**
- **Precision:** Marker-based AR offers high precision because it relies on known markers with predefined characteristics. - **Stability:** The tracking is usually stable and less prone to drift because the markers provide reliable reference points. - **Rich Interactions:** Marker-based AR allows for complex interactions and animations tied to specific markers.

**Use Cases for Marker-Based AR:**
- **Educational Apps:** Marker-based AR is often used in educational applications to provide interactive learning experiences. For example, pointing a mobile device at a textbook page with markers could trigger 3D models or additional information. - **Advertising and Promotion:** Companies use markers in print ads, posters, or product packaging to enhance

advertising campaigns. Scanning the marker with a mobile app can unlock special content or promotions. - **Entertainment:** Marker-based AR is used in gaming and entertainment, where markers can trigger augmented characters or animations in physical spaces. ### Markerless AR

**Markerless AR**, also known as **Location-Based AR**, doesn't rely on predefined markers. Instead, it uses the device's sensors, such as GPS, accelerometers, gyroscopes, and cameras, to understand the user's environment and position virtual objects accordingly. Here's how markerless AR works: 1. **Environmental Understanding:** Markerless AR systems build a digital understanding of the real-world environment. This includes recognizing objects, surfaces, and their positions. 2. **Sensor Fusion:** Data from various sensors, such as GPS for location, accelerometers for motion, and cameras for visual input, are combined to create a unified understanding of the user's surroundings. 3. **Object Recognition:** Markerless AR systems use computer vision and machine learning to recognize objects and surfaces. This can include recognizing walls, floors, and even furniture.

**Advantages of Markerless AR:**
- **No Need for Markers:** Markerless AR doesn't require predefined markers, making it more flexible for various environments. - **Natural Interaction:** It provides a more natural and immersive AR experience since it interacts with the real environment directly.

**Use Cases for Markerless AR:**
- **Navigation and Wayfinding:** Apps like Google Maps use markerless AR to provide directions and guide users through real-world locations. - **Real Estate and Interior Design:** Markerless AR is used to visualize furniture and interior design changes within a room by recognizing surfaces and objects. - **Gaming and Entertainment:** Location-based AR games like Pokémon GO use markerless techniques to place digital creatures in the real world.

In conclusion, both marker-based and markerless AR have their strengths and use cases. Marker-based AR is precise and stable, making it suitable for educational and advertising applications. On the other hand, markerless AR offers more flexibility and a natural interaction style, making it ideal for navigation, gaming, and interior design applications. The choice between these approaches depends on the specific requirements of the AR application and the user experience you want to deliver.

## Section 17.4: AR Content Creation

Creating content for Augmented Reality (AR) applications involves a unique set of considerations compared to traditional 2D or 3D content creation. In this section, we'll explore the key aspects of AR content creation, including the tools, techniques, and best practices involved. ### 1. 3D Modeling and Animation

AR often involves placing 3D objects or animations into the real world. Therefore, 3D modeling and animation tools are essential for AR content creation. Popular software includes Blender, Maya, 3ds Max, and Unity's built-in tools. Here's a simplified workflow for AR content creation: - **Modeling:** Create or import 3D models of objects or characters that will appear in the AR scene. - **Texturing:** Apply textures and materials to your 3D models to make them visually appealing. - **Rigging and Animation:** Rig 3D characters for animation and create animations for interactions. ### 2. Marker and Surface Recognition

Depending on your AR application, you may need to create markers or define how your content recognizes real-world surfaces. Tools like ARToolkit and Vuforia allow you to generate markers and define tracking behavior. ### 3. Unity and ARCore/ARKit

Unity is a widely used game engine that supports AR development. Unity's AR Foundation framework enables cross-platform AR app development using ARCore (for Android) and

ARKit (for iOS). It provides an AR-specific interface, making it easier to integrate AR content. ### 4. Interaction Design

Consider how users will interact with your AR content. Touch gestures, voice commands, and device motion can all be used for interaction. Ensure that interactions feel intuitive and enhance the overall user experience. ### 5. Testing and Iteration

Testing is a crucial part of AR content creation. Use AR simulators in development environments to preview how your content will behave in the real world. Conduct user testing to gather feedback and make improvements. ### 6. Optimization

AR content should be optimized for performance to ensure a smooth experience. This involves reducing polygon counts, optimizing textures, and managing memory efficiently. ### 7. Realism vs. Stylization

Decide whether your AR content should aim for realism or adopt a stylized look. The choice depends on the app's purpose and target audience. Realism requires more detailed modeling and textures, while stylization allows for more creative freedom. ### 8. Scalability

Consider how your AR content will scale across different devices and screen sizes. Ensure that it works well on a variety of smartphones and tablets. ### 9. Audio Integration

Don't forget the audio aspect of AR content. Incorporate sound effects, background music, and spatial audio to enhance the immersive experience. ### 10. Legal and Ethical Considerations

If your AR content involves real-world locations or copyrighted material, be aware of legal and ethical considerations. Ensure that you have the necessary permissions and rights to use certain content in your AR app.

In summary, AR content creation involves a combination of 3D modeling, animation, interaction design, and technical integration. The choice of tools and techniques depends on the specific requirements of your AR application. Successful AR content creators pay attention to realism, performance optimization, and user interaction while considering legal and ethical aspects. AR content creation is an exciting and evolving field with vast creative potential, making it an attractive area for developers and artists alike.

## Section 17.5: Integrating Graphics with Real-World Environments

Integrating computer-generated graphics with real-world environments is the essence of augmented reality (AR). In this section, we'll delve into the techniques and considerations for seamlessly blending virtual content into the physical world. ### 1. Tracking and Registration

A fundamental aspect of AR is tracking the user's device and aligning virtual content with the real world. This involves recognizing and registering real-world features or markers. Various tracking methods exist: - **Marker-Based Tracking:** AR markers, like QR codes, are placed in the environment. The app recognizes these markers and positions content relative to them. - **SLAM (Simultaneous Localization and Mapping):** SLAM technology tracks the device's movement while simultaneously creating a map of the surroundings. This is commonly used in mobile AR. ### 2. Markerless Tracking

Markerless tracking doesn't rely on predefined markers but instead uses computer vision techniques to understand the environment. It's more versatile but can be computationally intensive. Depth-sensing cameras, like those on some smartphones, aid in markerless tracking. ### 3. Object Recognition

Advanced AR apps can recognize and track specific objects or images. For example, pointing your device at a book cover might trigger an AR animation related to the book's content. ### 4. Geolocation

Some AR experiences are tied to specific GPS locations. Pokémon GO, for instance, uses geolocation to place creatures in real-world areas.

### 5. Lighting and Shading

To make virtual objects look natural in real-world lighting conditions, you need to consider lighting and shading. Unity's AR Foundation, for example, supports physically-based rendering (PBR) to achieve realistic lighting effects.

### 6. Occlusion

One of the most challenging aspects of AR is occlusion, where virtual objects are hidden by real-world objects. Advanced AR systems are starting to address this with depth-sensing cameras that can identify real-world geometry.

### 7. Interaction

AR content should respond to user interactions. This includes touch gestures, voice commands, and spatial gestures (like hand movements). ARCore and ARKit provide APIs for handling user input in AR apps.

### 8. Multi-Platform Development

Developing AR apps often involves targeting multiple platforms, such as iOS and Android. Tools like Unity's AR Foundation help in building cross-platform AR experiences.

### 9. Performance and Optimization

AR apps must run smoothly on a variety of devices. Performance optimization is crucial, and this includes optimizing 3D models, textures, and animations.

### 10. User Experience

A successful AR app pays attention to user experience. Content should be engaging, intuitive, and add value to the real world. User testing and feedback are vital for refining the experience.

### 11. Real-World Data Integration

AR apps can benefit from real-world data sources, such as weather or traffic information, to enhance the user experience. Integrating these data sources requires careful consideration of data accuracy and timeliness.

### 12. Privacy and Security

Collecting data from the real world and user interactions raises privacy and security concerns. AR app developers should adhere to best practices for data protection and user consent.

In summary, integrating graphics with real-world environments in AR applications is a complex and exciting endeavor. It involves tracking, recognition, lighting, interaction, and optimization, among other considerations. The goal is to create immersive and seamless experiences where virtual and real worlds coexist harmoniously, opening up numerous possibilities in fields like gaming, education, navigation, and more.

# Chapter 18: Future Trends in Graphics Programming

## Section 18.1: Ray Tracing in Real-Time Graphics

Ray tracing is a rendering technique that simulates the behavior of light rays as they interact with objects in a scene. Traditionally, ray tracing has been computationally intensive and primarily used for offline rendering, such as in movies and high-quality visual effects. However, recent developments have brought real-time ray tracing to the forefront of graphics programming. In this section, we'll explore the implications and advancements in real-time ray tracing. ### 1. Ray Tracing Basics

Ray tracing is based on the concept of casting rays from a camera into the scene and simulating how these rays interact with objects. It calculates the color of each pixel by tracing rays of light as they bounce around the scene, taking into account reflections, refractions, and shadows. ### 2. Real-Time Ray Tracing Hardware

The shift towards real-time ray tracing has been accelerated by the development of dedicated hardware. Graphics cards like NVIDIA's RTX series feature RT cores specifically designed for ray tracing operations, significantly improving performance. ### 3. Improved Visual Realism

Real-time ray tracing enables more realistic lighting, shadows, and reflections in games and simulations. It can simulate global illumination, soft shadows, and complex materials with greater fidelity than traditional rasterization techniques. ### 4. Hybrid Rendering

Many modern game engines are adopting a hybrid rendering approach that combines traditional rasterization with ray tracing. This allows developers to use ray tracing selectively for specific effects or scenes while maintaining real-time performance. ### 5. Game-Changing Applications

Real-time ray tracing has the potential to transform various industries beyond gaming, including architectural visualization, automotive design, and film production. It offers a level of realism that was previously unattainable in real-time applications. ### 6. Challenges and Optimization

Despite the hardware advancements, real-time ray tracing still poses challenges in terms of performance optimization. Developers need to implement techniques like denoising and efficient acceleration structures to achieve acceptable frame rates. ### 7. Emerging Ray Tracing APIs

APIs like NVIDIA's RTX and Microsoft's DirectX Raytracing (DXR) provide standardized interfaces for developers to implement real-time ray tracing in their applications. These APIs abstract the underlying hardware and make ray tracing more accessible. ### 8. The Future of Real-Time Graphics

Real-time ray tracing represents a significant step forward in graphics programming. As hardware continues to evolve, and developers become more proficient in optimizing ray tracing pipelines, we can expect even more realistic and immersive graphics in future games and applications.

In conclusion, real-time ray tracing is a game-changer in the world of graphics programming. It has the potential to revolutionize how we experience and interact with digital environments, and its applications extend far beyond gaming. As hardware and software support for ray tracing continue to grow, we can look forward to increasingly stunning and realistic visual experiences in various domains.

## Section 18.2: Machine Learning and Graphics

Machine learning (ML) has become an integral part of graphics programming, opening up exciting possibilities for creating more immersive and efficient graphics applications. In this section, we'll explore the intersection of machine learning and graphics and how it is shaping the future of the field. ### 1. ML for Image and Video Processing

Machine learning techniques, especially deep learning, have shown remarkable results in image and video processing tasks. ML models can enhance images, denoise them, remove artifacts, and even generate content. In graphics programming, this is valuable for improving the quality of textures, post-processing effects, and more. ### 2. Generative Models

Generative models like Generative Adversarial Networks (GANs) and Variational Autoencoders (VAEs) have gained popularity in graphics. GANs, for example, can generate realistic images, textures, and 3D models. This technology can be used for procedurally generating content in games, creating realistic characters, or even generating entire game worlds. ### 3. ML for Animation and Character Control

Machine learning has found applications in character animation and control. Reinforcement learning can be used to teach characters in games how to navigate and interact with their environment realistically. This can lead to more lifelike and dynamic character behavior. ### 4. Real-Time AI

Real-time AI, driven by machine learning, is being employed in games for creating adaptive and intelligent non-player characters (NPCs). These NPCs can adapt to the player's behavior, making gameplay more challenging and engaging. ### 5. ML in Content Creation

Content creation tools for graphics artists are also benefiting from ML. Software can assist artists in generating complex 3D models, generating textures, or automating repetitive tasks like rigging and skinning. ### 6. Training Data and Datasets

One of the critical aspects of using machine learning in graphics is the availability of large and diverse datasets. Training ML models often requires extensive data, and for graphics-related tasks, this includes high-quality images, 3D models, and animations. ### 7. Challenges and Ethical Considerations

As with any technology, there are challenges and ethical considerations. Bias in training data can lead to biased results, which is a concern in graphics, especially for applications like character generation. Ensuring fairness and diversity in training data is crucial. ### 8. Integration with Graphics APIs

ML frameworks and libraries are increasingly integrated with graphics APIs, making it easier for developers to incorporate machine learning into their graphics applications. This integration allows for real-time ML-powered graphics effects. ### 9. The Future of ML and Graphics

The synergy between machine learning and graphics is likely to continue to grow. As hardware becomes more capable and algorithms more sophisticated, we can expect even more impressive applications of machine learning in graphics programming. Whether it's creating more realistic game worlds, generating high-quality content, or enhancing user experiences, machine learning is a powerful tool for the future of graphics.

In summary, machine learning is revolutionizing graphics programming by enabling more realistic content generation, enhancing image and video processing, and creating intelligent, adaptive environments. As the field continues to evolve, it opens up new avenues for creativity and innovation in graphics and interactive experiences.

## Section 18.3: Quantum Computing and Graphics

Quantum computing is an emerging field with the potential to revolutionize various domains, including graphics programming. In this section, we will explore the intersection of quantum computing and graphics and discuss how quantum technologies may impact the future of graphics programming. ### 1. Quantum Computing Basics

Quantum computing leverages the principles of quantum mechanics to perform computations that would be infeasible for classical computers. Instead of using classical bits, quantum computers use quantum bits or qubits. Qubits can exist in multiple states simultaneously, which enables them to perform certain calculations exponentially faster than classical computers. ### 2. Quantum Graphics Algorithms

Quantum computing can potentially offer significant speedup in solving complex graphics-related problems. For instance, rendering photorealistic images and simulating global illumination in real-time are computationally intensive tasks. Quantum algorithms might provide more efficient solutions, leading to better graphics quality and performance. ### 3. Quantum Simulations

Quantum computers excel in simulating quantum systems, and this capability can be harnessed for simulating materials and physical phenomena in graphics. Quantum simulations can lead to more accurate and realistic physics-based rendering, benefiting applications like games and simulations. ### 4. Quantum Machine Learning

Quantum machine learning algorithms have the potential to enhance graphics tasks such as image recognition, denoising, and content generation. Quantum neural networks and quantum-enhanced feature extraction could improve the quality and speed of graphics-related ML tasks. ### 5. Challenges and Limitations

Despite its promise, quantum computing is still in its infancy, and there are several challenges to overcome. Quantum hardware is delicate and highly susceptible to errors. Developing quantum algorithms and software tools for graphics programming remains a complex and evolving field. ### 6. Quantum Hardware

The availability and accessibility of quantum hardware are increasing, but widespread adoption in graphics programming is not immediate. Graphics developers may need to adapt to quantum programming languages and frameworks. ### 7. Ethical Considerations

As quantum computing advances, ethical considerations related to its use in graphics programming will become important. Issues like data privacy, security, and the potential for misuse must be addressed. ### 8. Collaboration and Research

Collaboration between quantum computing researchers and graphics programmers is crucial for harnessing the potential of quantum technologies. Joint efforts can lead to the development of quantum algorithms tailored to graphics tasks and the integration of quantum computing into existing graphics pipelines. ### 9. The Future of Quantum Graphics

The integration of quantum computing into graphics programming is still in its early stages. However, as quantum technologies mature and become more accessible, we can expect quantum graphics algorithms and applications to advance. This may lead to breakthroughs in graphics quality, speed, and realism.

In conclusion, quantum computing holds the promise of transforming graphics programming by offering faster and more efficient algorithms for complex tasks. While it is an evolving field with challenges to overcome, the potential benefits for graphics, including rendering, simulation, and machine learning, make quantum computing an exciting area of exploration for the future of graphics programming. Collaboration, research, and ethical considerations will play vital roles in shaping the direction of quantum graphics.

## Section 18.4: Holographic Displays

Holographic displays represent a cutting-edge technology that has the potential to redefine the way we interact with digital content. In this section, we'll delve into the world of holographic displays, discussing their principles, applications, and impact on graphics programming. ### 1. Understanding Holographic Displays

Holographic displays create three-dimensional images that appear to exist in space without the need for special eyewear. Unlike traditional displays that are 2D, holographic displays offer true 3D visualization. This is achieved through the interference of light waves to reproduce the depth, parallax, and realism of objects. ### 2. Working Principles

Holographic displays use lasers or other coherent light sources to create interference patterns on a photosensitive surface such as a holographic plate or a spatial light modulator (SLM). These patterns are recorded and later illuminated with a reference beam to reconstruct the 3D image. ### 3. Applications in Graphics

Holographic displays have the potential to revolutionize graphics applications. They can enable the visualization of 3D models, data visualizations, and virtual environments with unprecedented realism. Graphics programmers can develop applications that take full advantage of the immersive nature of holographic displays. ### 4. Challenges in Holographic Graphics

Despite their potential, holographic displays present challenges for graphics programming. Generating high-quality holographic content demands significant computational power and advanced algorithms. Optimizing graphics pipelines for real-time holographic rendering is a complex task. ### 5. Mixed Reality (MR) Integration

Holographic displays are often integrated into mixed reality (MR) headsets, combining holographic and real-world elements. Graphics programmers working on MR applications must consider spatial mapping, gesture recognition, and interaction design to create compelling experiences. ### 6. Content Creation Tools

The development of content creation tools for holographic displays is essential. Graphics software needs to support the creation and manipulation of holographic assets and animations. This includes 3D modeling, texturing, and animation tools tailored for holographic content. ### 7. Future Potential

Holographic displays have the potential to transform a wide range of industries, including gaming, education, healthcare, and design. Graphics programmers will play a crucial role in harnessing this technology to create innovative applications and experiences. ### 8. Ethical and Privacy Considerations

As with any emerging technology, holographic displays raise ethical and privacy concerns. Graphics programmers must consider issues related to data privacy, security, and the potential misuse of holographic content. ### 9. Collaboration and Research

Collaboration between graphics programmers, hardware engineers, and researchers is vital for advancing holographic display technology. Research efforts can lead to more efficient algorithms, better hardware, and improved user experiences. ### 10. Conclusion

Holographic displays represent a promising frontier in graphics programming. While they pose challenges, the potential for immersive 3D visualization and interaction is immense. Graphics programmers have the opportunity to shape the future of holographic content creation and application development, making this an exciting field to watch as it continues to evolve.

## Section 18.5: Ethical and Environmental Considerations in Graphics

In the realm of graphics programming, it's essential to consider both ethical and environmental aspects. As technology advances, the impact of graphics on society and the environment becomes more significant. This section explores the ethical considerations and environmental implications of graphics programming. ### 1. Ethical Considerations #### a. Content and Accessibility

Graphics programmers are responsible for creating content that is inclusive and accessible to a diverse audience. This involves ensuring that graphics, user interfaces, and virtual environments are designed with considerations for people with disabilities. #### b. Privacy and Data Security

Graphics applications often collect and process user data. It's crucial to prioritize user privacy and data security, implementing robust measures to protect sensitive information and adhere to data protection regulations. #### c. Ethical Use of Technology

Graphics programmers should be mindful of the ethical use of technology. This includes avoiding the creation of content that promotes harm, discrimination, or illegal activities. Responsible use of graphics technology contributes to a safer and more inclusive digital landscape. #### d. Bias and Fairness

Algorithms used in graphics applications can inadvertently perpetuate bias and discrimination. Graphics programmers must be aware of these biases and work to mitigate them, ensuring fair and equitable outcomes. ### 2. Environmental Considerations #### a. Energy Efficiency

Graphics-intensive applications, such as video games and simulations, can consume significant amounts of energy, contributing to carbon emissions. Optimizing graphics rendering pipelines for energy efficiency helps reduce the environmental impact of these applications. #### b. Hardware Lifespan

The rapid advancement of graphics hardware can lead to the premature disposal of older devices, contributing to electronic waste. Graphics programmers can extend the lifespan of hardware by optimizing software to run efficiently on a wide range of devices. #### c. Sustainable Design

Sustainable design principles can be applied to graphics programming. This involves creating graphics assets and environments that minimize resource usage and carbon footprint. Using efficient compression formats, texture streaming, and LOD (Level of Detail) techniques can reduce the size and processing power required for rendering. #### d. Remote Work and Reduced Travel

Graphics technology can facilitate remote collaboration and virtual meetings, reducing the need for physical travel. This has the potential to lower carbon emissions associated with commuting and business travel. ### 3. Collaboration and Responsibility

Addressing ethical and environmental considerations in graphics programming requires collaboration among developers, designers, and stakeholders. It's a shared responsibility to create technology that benefits society while minimizing its negative impact on the environment and individuals. ### 4. Conclusion

As graphics programming continues to evolve, so too must our awareness of the ethical and environmental implications of our work. By adopting responsible practices and staying informed about emerging issues, graphics programmers can contribute to a more sustainable and ethically conscious digital future.

# Chapter 19: Graphics Programming Case Studies

## Section 19.1: Game Development Case Study

In this section, we delve into a comprehensive case study of game development using graphics programming techniques. Game development is one of the most prominent and demanding applications of graphics programming, involving various aspects such as rendering, physics simulation, audio, and gameplay mechanics. In this case study, we'll explore the development of a 3D action-adventure game called "EpicQuest." ### 1. Game Concept and Design #### a. Story and World Building

The first step in game development is to define the game's concept and design. In the case of "EpicQuest," we've created a rich fantasy world with a compelling storyline, a diverse cast of characters, and immersive environments. #### b. Gameplay Mechanics

Gameplay mechanics define how players interact with the game. "EpicQuest" features real-time combat, puzzle-solving, character progression, and exploration. The game's design focuses on delivering an engaging and rewarding player experience.

### 2. Graphics Rendering

#### a. Graphics Engine

A custom graphics engine is essential for creating the visual aspects of the game. "EpicQuest" utilizes a graphics engine that supports rendering 3D models, dynamic lighting, and special effects. We'll discuss the techniques used to achieve stunning visuals.

#### b. Asset Creation

Creating 3D models, textures, animations, and other assets is a critical aspect of game development. We'll explore the tools and workflows used to generate high-quality assets for "EpicQuest."

### 3. Physics Simulation

#### a. Character Physics

Realistic character movement and physics are crucial for immersion. We'll cover the implementation of character physics, including collision detection, character controllers, and ragdoll physics.

#### b. Environmental Physics

The game world in "EpicQuest" features dynamic environments with destructible objects and physics-based puzzles. We'll examine the physics simulation techniques employed to create interactive and believable environments.

### 4. Audio and Sound Design

#### a. Sound Effects

Sound effects play a vital role in enhancing gameplay and immersion. We'll discuss the creation and integration of sound effects, including footsteps, combat sounds, and environmental audio.

#### b. Music Composition

A captivating soundtrack contributes significantly to the game's atmosphere. We'll explore the process of composing and integrating music that complements the game's narrative and gameplay.

### 5. Gameplay Programming

#### a. AI and Enemy Behavior

Creating challenging AI opponents is essential for an action-adventure game. We'll delve into AI programming techniques used to design enemy behaviors, including pathfinding, decision-making, and combat strategies. #### b. Quest and Dialogue Systems

In "EpicQuest," quests and dialogues are integral to the story. We'll examine the implementation of quest systems, dialogue trees, and character interactions to drive the narrative forward. ### 6. Testing and Optimization #### a. Playtesting

Playtesting and user feedback are crucial for refining gameplay and identifying issues. We'll discuss the playtesting process and how it influenced the game's development. #### b. Performance Optimization

Optimizing performance is essential to ensure smooth gameplay on a variety of hardware configurations. We'll explore the techniques used to optimize rendering, physics, and resource management in "EpicQuest." ### 7. Release and Post-Launch #### a. Distribution Platforms

Choosing the right distribution platforms, such as Steam, console stores, or mobile app stores, is a critical decision. We'll discuss the considerations for platform selection and the process of releasing the game. #### b. Updates and Community Engagement

Continuing to support the game post-launch involves releasing updates, addressing player feedback, and engaging with the community. We'll explore strategies for maintaining an active player base and fostering a dedicated player community. ### 8. Conclusion

The "EpicQuest" case study provides an in-depth look at the development of a 3D action-adventure game using graphics programming techniques. Game development is a complex and multifaceted process, and this case study serves as a valuable resource for aspiring game developers and graphics programmers.

## Section 19.2: Simulation and Training Applications

In this section, we explore the application of graphics programming in the context of simulation and training. Simulations have a wide range of uses, from training pilots and astronauts to simulating the behavior of complex systems in scientific research. Graphics programming plays a crucial role in creating realistic and interactive simulations. We'll discuss the key aspects of developing simulation and training applications and highlight some real-world examples. ### 1. Simulation and Training Objectives

Simulation and training applications aim to replicate real-world scenarios and environments for various purposes, including: - **Training** : Simulators are used to train professionals in fields such as aviation, healthcare, and military operations. These simulations provide a safe and controlled environment for trainees to practice their skills. - **Research** : Simulations are essential tools in scientific research. They allow scientists and researchers to model and study complex phenomena, such as climate systems, particle physics, and fluid dynamics. - **Testing and Validation** : Simulations can be used to test the behavior of systems and validate their performance. This is common in engineering and product development. ### 2. Realistic Rendering

Creating realistic visuals is a fundamental aspect of simulation and training applications. Graphics programming techniques are used to render 3D models, environments, and visual effects. Achieving realism involves: - **High-Quality Models** : Detailed 3D models of objects, vehicles, and environments are created to mimic real-world counterparts accurately. - **Realistic Lighting** : Advanced lighting models are employed to simulate the interaction of light with surfaces, resulting in realistic shadows, reflections, and highlights. - **Texture Mapping** : Textures are used to add surface details, such as bump maps, specular maps, and diffuse textures, to enhance realism. - **Particle Systems** : Simulations often include particle systems for effects like fire, smoke, water, and explosions. ### 3. Physics Simulation

Physics simulation is critical for accurate behavior in training applications. Whether it's simulating the dynamics of a flight simulator or the behavior of a medical instrument, physics engines are employed to model: - **Collision Detection** : Ensuring that objects interact realistically, collide, and respond to forces accurately. - **Fluid Dynamics** : Simulating the flow of liquids and gases for applications like fluid training and environmental modeling. - **Rigid Body Dynamics** : Modeling the movement of solid objects with consideration of mass, friction, and inertia. ### 4. User Interaction

User interaction is another vital aspect of simulation and training applications. Providing intuitive and realistic interaction is essential. This includes: - **Input Devices** : Integration of specialized input devices such as joysticks, motion controllers, and haptic feedback devices for realistic user input. - **User Interfaces** : Designing user interfaces that facilitate control and interaction within the simulation environment. ### 5. Scenario Development

In simulation and training applications, scenarios are designed to meet specific training objectives. Scenario development involves: - **Scenario Scripting** : Creating scripted sequences of events, scenarios, and training exercises. - **Scenario Customization** : Allowing users to customize scenarios and training parameters to suit their needs. ### 6. Case Studies

Real-world examples of simulation and training applications include: - **Flight Simulators** : Used for pilot training, aircraft maintenance training, and aviation research. - **Medical Simulators** : Used for training healthcare professionals in surgical procedures and patient care. - **Military Training Simulators** : Employed for military personnel training, including combat scenarios and equipment operation. - **Engineering Simulations** : Applied in product development and testing, including automotive crash simulations and structural analysis. - **Scientific Simulations** : Used in research for modeling complex phenomena, such as climate modeling and astrophysics simulations.

In conclusion, simulation and training applications leverage graphics programming to create immersive and realistic environments for training and research purposes. These applications are vital across various domains, ensuring safety, skill development, and scientific advancements. Graphics programming continues to play a significant role in pushing the boundaries of what is possible in the world of simulations.

## Section 19.3: Medical Visualization

Medical visualization is a field of graphics programming that focuses on creating visual representations of medical data for diagnostic, educational, and research purposes. It plays a crucial role in modern healthcare, enabling healthcare professionals to better understand complex medical data and aiding in diagnosis, treatment planning, and medical research. In this section, we will explore the key aspects of medical visualization and how graphics programming contributes to this important field. ### 1. Types of Medical Data

Medical data comes in various forms, including: - **Medical Images** : These include X-rays, CT scans, MRI images, ultrasound scans, and more. Each type of image has its unique characteristics and requires specialized visualization techniques. - **3D Models** : Medical professionals often need 3D models of organs, tissues, and anatomical structures for surgical planning and education. - **Patient Records** : Electronic health records (EHRs) and patient data, such as lab results and vital signs, can be visualized for better tracking and analysis. ### 2. Importance of Medical Visualization

Medical visualization offers several benefits: - **Diagnosis** : It aids in the accurate diagnosis of diseases and conditions by providing clear visual representations of medical data. - **Treatment Planning** : Surgeons use medical visualization to plan complex surgeries and interventions, reducing risks and improving outcomes. - **Patient Education** : Visualizations help patients understand their medical conditions and treatment options. - **Research** : Medical researchers use visualization to analyze and explore large datasets, identify patterns, and develop new treatments and therapies. ### 3. Graphics Programming in Medical Visualization

Graphics programming techniques are crucial in medical visualization for the following reasons: - **Image Processing** : Graphics programming allows for advanced image processing techniques, such as image enhancement, segmentation, and registration, to improve the quality and accuracy of medical images. - **3D Rendering** : Creating 3D models of anatomical structures and organs is essential for surgical planning. Graphics programming is used to render these models in real-time, allowing for interactive exploration. - **Volume Rendering** : Techniques like volume rendering are employed to visualize 3D medical data, such as CT and MRI scans. This provides a more comprehensive view of internal structures. - **Virtual Reality (VR) and Augmented Reality (AR)** : VR and AR technologies are increasingly used in medical visualization to provide immersive experiences for medical professionals and students. Graphics programming is essential for rendering 3D scenes in VR and AR environments. ### 4. Software Tools and Libraries

Several software tools and libraries are used in medical visualization, including: - **DICOM (Digital Imaging and Communications in Medicine)** : A standard for storing and transmitting medical images. Many medical imaging software tools support DICOM. - **VTK (Visualization Toolkit)** : An open-source library for 3D computer graphics, image processing, and visualization, widely used in medical applications. - **OpenGL** : The OpenGL API is used for real-time 3D rendering in medical visualization software and applications. - **Unity3D and Unreal Engine** : Game engines like Unity and Unreal Engine are increasingly used in medical visualization, thanks to their powerful graphics capabilities. ### 5. Case Studies

Real-world examples of medical visualization applications include: - **Surgical Planning** : Surgeons use 3D models and VR simulations to plan complex surgeries, such as craniofacial reconstruction. - **Diagnostic Tools** : Radiologists use specialized software to analyze and interpret medical images, improving the accuracy of diagnoses. - **Medical Education** : Medical students and professionals use interactive 3D models and VR simulations for training and education. - **Drug Discovery** : Researchers use visualization techniques to analyze the interactions between drugs and biological molecules, aiding in drug discovery.

In conclusion, medical visualization is a critical field that relies heavily on graphics programming to provide valuable insights into medical data. It enhances diagnosis, treatment planning, and medical research, ultimately improving patient care and outcomes. Graphics programming continues to play a pivotal role in advancing medical visualization technologies and applications.

## Section 19.4: Architectural Visualization

Architectural visualization is a specialized field within the broader realm of graphics programming that focuses on creating visual representations of architectural designs and structures. This field serves a crucial role in architecture, construction, and real estate by allowing architects, designers, and clients to visualize and understand building concepts before construction begins. In this section, we will explore the key aspects of architectural visualization and the role of graphics programming in this field. ### 1. Importance of Architectural Visualization

Architectural visualization offers several advantages: - **Design Exploration** : It enables architects and designers to experiment with various design concepts and make informed decisions before committing to a particular design. - **Client Communication** : Visualizations help architects and clients communicate and ensure that the client's vision aligns with the architect's design. - **Error Detection** : Visualization can reveal design flaws or construction issues early in the process, saving time and resources. - **Marketing and Sales** : Real estate developers use visualizations to market properties before they are built, attracting potential buyers and investors. ### 2. Types of Architectural Visualizations

Architectural visualizations come in various forms, including: - **Rendered Images** : High-quality rendered images provide a photorealistic view of the architectural design, including lighting, materials, and surroundings. - **Virtual Tours** : Interactive virtual tours allow users to explore the building's interior and exterior in real-time. - **3D Models** : Detailed 3D models of the architectural design provide a comprehensive view of the structure from various angles. - **Augmented Reality (AR)** : AR applications overlay digital architectural elements onto the real-world environment using smartphones or AR glasses. - **Virtual Reality (VR)** : VR environments immerse users in a virtual representation of the architectural design, enabling a more immersive experience. ### 3. Graphics Programming in Architectural Visualization

Graphics programming plays a pivotal role in architectural visualization for the following reasons: - **Realistic Rendering** : Graphics programmers use techniques such as ray tracing and physically-based rendering (PBR) to create highly realistic visualizations with accurate lighting, shadows, and materials. - **Interactivity** : Interactive visualizations and VR experiences require real-time rendering and responsive user interactions, which are made possible through graphics programming. - **Efficient Data Handling** : Large architectural models with intricate details require efficient data handling and rendering optimizations to maintain smooth performance. - **Cross-Platform Compatibility** : Architects and clients may use various devices and platforms, necessitating cross-platform compatibility, which graphics programmers ensure. ### 4. Software Tools and Libraries

Several software tools and libraries are commonly used in architectural visualization: - **AutoCAD** : Architects use AutoCAD for creating 2D and 3D architectural drawings and plans. - **SketchUp** : SketchUp is a popular tool for creating 3D models and architectural designs. - **Blender** : Blender is a versatile open-source 3D modeling and animation software that can be used for architectural visualization. - **Unity3D and Unreal Engine** : Game engines like Unity and Unreal Engine are employed to create interactive architectural visualizations and VR experiences. - **Enscape** : Enscape is a real-time rendering and virtual reality plugin for architectural design software, providing instant visual feedback. ### 5. Case Studies

Architectural visualization is widely used in the architecture and real estate industries: - **Pre-Construction Visualization** : Architects use 3D models and renderings to showcase their designs to clients and investors, helping secure project funding. - **Real Estate Marketing** : Developers create VR tours and renderings to market properties, allowing potential buyers to explore them virtually. - **Interior Design** : Interior designers use visualization to experiment with different layouts, colors, and furniture arrangements. - **Historical Preservation** : Visualization can be used to recreate and preserve historical structures or landmarks digitally.

In summary, architectural visualization is a critical aspect of architecture and construction, aiding in design exploration, client communication, error detection, and marketing. Graphics programming enables the creation of realistic and interactive visualizations, contributing to better decision-making and improved project outcomes in the architectural and real estate industries.

## Section 19.5: Scientific Visualization

Scientific visualization is a specialized field within graphics programming that focuses on creating visual representations of complex scientific data and phenomena. This field is essential for researchers, scientists, and engineers working in various disciplines, such as astronomy, geophysics, biology, and medicine. In this section, we will explore the significance of scientific visualization and the role of graphics programming in making sense of complex scientific data. ### 1. The Importance of Scientific Visualization

Scientific visualization serves several crucial purposes: - **Data Exploration** : It allows scientists to explore large and intricate datasets, uncover patterns, and gain insights that may not be evident in raw data. - **Communication** : Visualizations make it easier to convey complex scientific findings to colleagues, students, and the general public. - **Hypothesis Testing** : Researchers can test hypotheses visually by observing data trends and correlations. - **Simulation Results** : Scientific simulations, such as weather forecasting or fluid dynamics, produce vast datasets that require visualization for interpretation. - **Medical Imaging** : In medicine, visualization techniques are used for tasks like medical image analysis, surgical planning, and drug discovery. ### 2. Types of Scientific Visualizations

Scientific visualizations come in various forms, depending on the nature of the data and the goals of the analysis: - **2D and 3D Plots** : Simple plots and graphs are used to visualize data distributions, trends, and relationships. - **Volume Rendering** : This technique is employed to visualize 3D scalar fields, such as medical CT scans or fluid flow simulations. - **Isosurface Extraction** : Isosurfaces represent regions where a scalar field has a constant value, aiding in the visualization of complex structures. - **Particle Tracing** : This method visualizes the motion and behavior of particles within a simulation or dataset, such as tracking airflow in a room. - **Flow Visualization** : Used in fluid dynamics and aerodynamics, flow visualization techniques show the behavior of fluids, revealing vortices and turbulence. ### 3. Graphics Programming in Scientific Visualization

Graphics programming is fundamental in scientific visualization for the following reasons: - **Data Transformation** : Graphics programmers transform raw scientific data into visual representations using algorithms and techniques tailored to the specific dataset. - **Interactivity** : Interactive visualization tools allow researchers to explore data dynamically, adjust parameters, and gain insights in real time. - **Performance Optimization** : High-performance computing and GPU acceleration are crucial for handling large datasets and rendering complex visualizations efficiently. - **Visual Quality** :

Graphics programmers use techniques like shading, transparency, and lighting to enhance the visual quality and interpretability of scientific visualizations. ### 4. Software Tools and Libraries

Several software tools and libraries are widely used in scientific visualization: - **Matplotlib** : Matplotlib is a popular Python library for creating static, animated, and interactive 2D and 3D plots. - **ParaView** : ParaView is an open-source, cross-platform data analysis and visualization tool designed for large datasets. - **VTK (Visualization Toolkit)** : VTK is an open-source library for 3D computer graphics, image processing, and visualization. - **Visit** : Visit is a visualization and analysis tool designed for the examination of 2D and 3D scientific data. - **Amira-Avizo** : These commercial software packages are used for 3D visualization and analysis of scientific data, especially in the life sciences. ### 5. Case Studies

Scientific visualization has numerous applications across scientific domains: - **Astronomy** : Astronomers use visualization to study celestial objects, simulate cosmic phenomena, and communicate their findings to the public. - **Climate Modeling** : Climate scientists use visualizations to understand climate patterns, project future scenarios, and inform policymakers. - **Biomedical Imaging** : Medical researchers rely on visualization for tasks like studying the human brain's structure, visualizing DNA structures, and tracking the progression of diseases. - **Geophysics** : Geophysicists use visualization to analyze seismic data, map subsurface structures, and monitor geological processes. - **Material Science** : Researchers in material science visualize atomic and molecular structures to design new materials with specific properties.

In summary, scientific visualization is an indispensable tool for scientists and researchers across various disciplines. Graphics programming enables the creation of meaningful visualizations, aiding in data exploration, communication, hypothesis testing, and scientific discovery. As datasets continue to grow in complexity, the role of graphics programming in scientific visualization becomes increasingly vital.

# Chapter 20: Conclusion and Beyond

## Section 20.1: Recap of Key Concepts

In this concluding chapter, we will summarize the key concepts and takeaways from this book on graphics programming. We'll revisit the fundamental ideas, techniques, and best practices discussed throughout the book, providing a comprehensive overview of what you've learned. ### 1. Graphics Programming Fundamentals

We began our journey with an introduction to graphics programming, understanding the significance of graphics APIs, and exploring the evolution of OpenGL and Vulkan. We discussed setting up the development environment and delved into the basics of 2D and 3D rendering, equipping you with a strong foundation. ### 2. Advanced Techniques and Optimization

Chapter 3 introduced advanced OpenGL techniques, including lighting, shading, texturing, and 3D model implementation. We then dived into Vulkan, learning about its low-level approach, command buffers, pipelines, and memory management. Optimizing graphics performance, profiling, and validation layers were key themes in Chapter 8. ### 3. Cross-Platform Development and Best Practices

Cross-platform development (Chapter 9) explored the importance of targeting multiple platforms and handling input and windowing. Chapter 10 emphasized coding standards, version control, documentation, continuous integration, and staying updated with graphics API changes. ### 4. Advanced Graphics Effects

Chapter 11 delved into advanced graphics effects, such as real-time ray tracing, global illumination, procedural texture generation, and post-processing effects. We also discussed integrating graphics into virtual reality (VR) and augmented reality (AR) applications. ### 5. Graphics and Game Engines

Chapter 12 provided an overview of game engines and how to integrate OpenGL and Vulkan with them. We explored the development of a simple game engine and discussed physics simulations and audio in games. ### 6. 2D Graphics and GUI Development

Chapter 13 focused on 2D graphics and GUI development, including building 2D games, GUI design and implementation, user input handling, animations, and debugging and profiling. ### 7. Debugging and Optimization Tools

Chapter 14 introduced GPU debugging and profiling tools, CPU profiling and optimization, graphics debugging techniques, performance analysis tools, and troubleshooting common graphics issues. ### 8. Graphics Programming Challenges

Chapter 15 discussed tackling challenges like handling large worlds and terrain, real-time fluid simulation, cloth simulation, implementing AI and pathfinding, and networked multiplayer graphics. ### 9. Graphics in Virtual and Augmented Reality

Chapters 16 and 17 covered graphics in virtual reality (VR) and augmented reality (AR), including VR headsets, tracking, rendering techniques, interaction, and challenges in VR and AR graphics. ### 10. Future Trends and Case Studies

Chapter 18 explored future trends in graphics programming, such as real-time ray tracing, machine learning, quantum computing, holographic displays, and ethical/environmental considerations. Chapter 19 presented case studies in game development, simulation, medical visualization, architectural visualization, and scientific visualization. ### 11. Conclusion and Beyond

In this final chapter, we've revisited the breadth of knowledge gained in this book. Graphics programming is a dynamic and ever-evolving field, and your journey doesn't end here. There are always new techniques, technologies, and challenges to explore. As you continue your graphics programming endeavors, remember to stay curious, engaged, and connected to the graphics programming community. The resources for further learning are abundant, and your contributions to this exciting field can shape its future.

Congratulations on completing this comprehensive guide to graphics programming!

## Section 20.2: The Journey Ahead

As we conclude this book on graphics programming, it's important to look ahead at the journey that lies in front of you. The world of graphics programming is vast and continually evolving, and there are many avenues you can explore to further enhance your skills and contribute to this exciting field. ### 1. Specialization and Expertise

Consider specializing in a specific area of graphics programming that aligns with your interests and career goals. Whether it's real-time rendering, game engine development, virtual reality, augmented reality, or any other aspect of graphics, becoming an expert in a niche can open up unique opportunities. ### 2. Keeping Up with Advances

Graphics programming is a field where technological advancements happen rapidly. Stay up-to-date with the latest developments in graphics hardware and software. Follow blogs, forums, and academic research to remain informed about emerging techniques and technologies. ### 3. Contribution to Open Source

Contributing to open-source graphics projects can be a valuable way to both learn and give back to the community. You can work on open-source game engines, rendering libraries, or tools, collaborating with developers from around the world. ### 4. Advanced Education

Consider pursuing advanced degrees or courses in computer graphics, computer science, or related fields. Formal education can provide you with in-depth knowledge and research opportunities. ### 5. Research and Innovation

Graphics programming often intersects with cutting-edge technologies like ray tracing, machine learning, and quantum computing. Exploring research and innovation in these areas can lead to breakthroughs in graphics technology. ### 6. Game Development

If you're passionate about game development, consider working on indie game projects or joining established game development studios. Creating games allows you to apply your graphics programming skills in a creative and tangible way. ### 7. Collaborative Projects

Collaborate with fellow graphics programmers on projects of mutual interest. Teamwork can lead to innovative solutions and expand your network in the graphics community. ### 8. Teaching and Mentorship

Share your knowledge by teaching or mentoring others interested in graphics programming. Whether it's through workshops, online courses, or one-on-one guidance, helping others learn can be fulfilling. ### 9. Graphics Community Engagement

Engage with the graphics programming community by attending conferences, meetups, and online forums. Networking with professionals in the field can lead to new opportunities and insights. ### 10. Ethical Considerations

As graphics technology advances, it's essential to consider its ethical implications. Think about how your work in graphics programming can be used responsibly and ethically, especially in areas like AI, VR, and AR.

Remember that the journey in graphics programming is not linear. It's full of challenges, discoveries, and opportunities for growth. Whether you're a beginner or an experienced programmer, the world of graphics programming offers a multitude of exciting paths to explore. Embrace the journey ahead with curiosity, enthusiasm, and a passion for creating stunning visual experiences.

## Section 20.3: Resources for Further Learning

In your journey through the world of graphics programming, it's crucial to have access to quality learning resources. Here, we'll explore various resources that can help you continue your education and stay updated in this dynamic field. ### 1. Online Tutorials and Courses

Online platforms like Coursera, edX, Udemy, and Khan Academy offer a wide range of graphics programming courses. These courses cater to different skill levels, from beginners to advanced programmers. You can explore topics like OpenGL, Vulkan, DirectX, and more. ### 2. Books and Documentation

Books are an excellent resource for in-depth knowledge. Consider reading advanced graphics programming books and official documentation for graphics APIs. They provide detailed insights and examples that can enhance your understanding. ### 3. Academic Journals and Papers

Stay current with the latest research in graphics programming by reading academic journals and research papers. Websites like ACM Digital Library and IEEE Xplore host a wealth of papers on computer graphics, rendering, and related topics. ### 4. Forums and Communities

Engage with graphics programming communities on platforms like Stack Overflow, Reddit's r/GraphicsProgramming, and specialized forums like OpenGL.org. These communities can be invaluable for troubleshooting, sharing knowledge, and staying informed about industry trends. ### 5. GitHub and Open Source Projects

Explore open-source graphics projects on GitHub. Contributing to or studying the source code of these projects can provide practical insights into graphics programming techniques and best practices. ### 6. Graphics Programming Blogs

Many experienced graphics programmers maintain blogs where they share their knowledge and experiences. These blogs often contain tutorials, code samples, and insights into solving real-world graphics challenges. ### 7. YouTube and Video Tutorials

Video tutorials on platforms like YouTube can be an engaging way to learn graphics programming. Many educators and developers create video content covering various graphics topics. ### 8. University Courses

Consider enrolling in university-level courses related to computer graphics or game development. Many universities offer online courses, allowing you to access quality education from anywhere in the world. ### 9. Conferences and Meetups

Participate in graphics-related conferences and meetups to network with professionals, attend talks, and learn about the latest advancements in the field. Conferences like SIGGRAPH and GDC are renowned in the industry. ### 10. Online Coding Challenges

Platforms like LeetCode and HackerRank offer coding challenges that can sharpen your problem-solving skills, which are valuable in graphics programming. ### 11. Graphics Programming Libraries

Explore graphics programming libraries like OpenGL, Vulkan, DirectX, and WebGL. Experiment with sample code and documentation provided by these libraries to gain hands-on experience. ### 12. Social Media and Subreddits

Follow graphics programming-related accounts on Twitter and join subreddits dedicated to graphics. These platforms often share news, articles, and discussions related to the field. ### 13. Specialized Courses and Certifications

Consider specialized courses and certifications in areas like game development, real-time rendering, or VR/AR development. These credentials can enhance your resume and demonstrate expertise. ### 14. Industry Publications

Keep an eye on industry publications, such as websites and magazines focused on graphics and game development. They often feature articles, interviews, and insights from professionals in the field.

Remember that learning is an ongoing process, and the field of graphics programming is ever-evolving. Explore a combination of these resources to tailor your learning experience to your specific interests and career goals. Stay curious, practice regularly, and don't be afraid to dive into challenging projects to deepen your understanding of graphics programming.

## Section 20.4: Joining the Graphics Programming Community

One of the most valuable aspects of being in the field of graphics programming is the sense of community. Engaging with the graphics programming community can open up numerous opportunities for learning, collaboration, and career growth. In this section, we'll explore how to become an active member of this community. ### 1. Online Forums and Communities

Joining online forums and communities dedicated to graphics programming is an excellent way to connect with like-minded individuals. Websites like Stack Overflow, Reddit's r/GraphicsProgramming, and specialized forums like OpenGL.org are popular platforms for discussions and problem-solving. ### 2. Attend Conferences and Meetups

Participating in graphics-related conferences and local meetups can be incredibly rewarding. Conferences like SIGGRAPH and GDC are renowned in the industry for networking, attending talks, and staying updated on the latest trends. Look for local meetups related to graphics programming in your area or participate in virtual events. ### 3. Engage on Social Media

Follow graphics programming-related accounts on platforms like Twitter and LinkedIn. These platforms often share news, articles, and discussions related to the field. Engaging in discussions and sharing your own insights can help you connect with professionals. ### 4. Contribute to Open Source Projects

Many open-source graphics projects welcome contributions from the community. Contributing to such projects not only allows you to give back but also provides you with real-world experience and a chance to collaborate with experienced developers. ### 5. Collaborate on GitHub

GitHub is a hub for graphics-related repositories and projects. Explore repositories, fork them, submit pull requests, or even start your own projects. GitHub offers an excellent platform for collaboration and learning from others. ### 6. Share Your Knowledge

Consider starting a blog, creating video tutorials, or giving presentations about graphics programming topics you're passionate about. Sharing your knowledge can help others and establish your expertise in the field. ### 7. Join Professional Organizations

Consider becoming a member of professional organizations related to graphics programming. These organizations often provide access to exclusive resources, networking opportunities, and events. ### 8. Attend Workshops and Training

Look for workshops and training programs related to graphics programming. These events often provide hands-on experience and access to experts who can guide your learning journey. ### 9. Mentorship and Mentorship Programs

Both offering and seeking mentorship can be incredibly beneficial. Experienced professionals can provide guidance, answer questions, and help you navigate your career path in graphics programming. ### 10. Hackathons and Game Jams

Participate in hackathons and game jams focused on graphics and game development. These events challenge you to apply your skills to create projects within a short timeframe, fostering creativity and problem-solving. ### 11. Academic Collaborations

If you're interested in research or advanced topics, consider collaborating with academic institutions or researchers in the field of computer graphics. These collaborations can lead to cutting-edge discoveries and innovations. ### 12. Stay Informed

Subscribe to newsletters, podcasts, and industry publications to stay informed about the latest developments in graphics programming. Being up-to-date is crucial in this rapidly evolving field.

Becoming an active member of the graphics programming community is not only about personal growth but also about contributing to the collective knowledge and advancement of the field. By engaging with others who share your passion, you'll have the opportunity to learn, share, and make a meaningful impact in the world of graphics programming.

## Section 20.5: Acknowledgments and Author's Note

As we come to the conclusion of this comprehensive guide on graphics programming, it's essential to acknowledge the contributions and express gratitude to all those who made this journey possible. In this final section, we'll also include an author's note to reflect on the writing process and the significance of this work. ### Acknowledgments

Writing a book of this magnitude would not have been possible without the support and expertise of many individuals. We would like to express our sincere gratitude to: 1. **Readers and Learners** : To all the readers and learners who have embarked on this graphics programming journey with us, thank you for your dedication to mastering this complex and exciting field. 2. **Contributors** : To the experts, developers, and contributors who shared their knowledge, insights, and code snippets to enhance the content of this book, your input has been invaluable. 3. **Reviewers and Editors** : To the diligent reviewers and editors who meticulously combed through the manuscript, ensuring accuracy and clarity, your efforts have elevated the quality of this work. 4. **Open Source and Graphics Communities** : To the open-source graphics communities, forums, and platforms that fostered a collaborative spirit and provided a wealth of resources, we are indebted for your support. 5. **Friends and Family** : To our friends and family members who offered unwavering encouragement, patience, and understanding during the long hours spent researching, writing, and editing, your support is deeply appreciated. ### Author's Note

Writing this book on graphics programming has been a labor of love, fueled by a passion for the subject matter and a commitment to sharing knowledge. Throughout the journey, we've strived to create a resource that not only imparts technical expertise but also inspires curiosity and creativity in the world of graphics.

Graphics programming is a dynamic and ever-evolving field, and this book serves as a snapshot of the knowledge available at the time of writing. We encourage readers to continue exploring, experimenting, and pushing the boundaries of what's possible in the realm of computer graphics.

The graphics programming community is vibrant, welcoming, and full of opportunities for collaboration and innovation. Whether you're a seasoned professional or just beginning your journey, know that you are part of a community that values learning, sharing, and pushing the boundaries of visual computing.

As technology advances and new horizons emerge, we hope this book remains a valuable reference and source of inspiration. The world of graphics programming is limitless, and we look forward to seeing the incredible creations and innovations that you, the reader, will contribute in the years to come.

Thank you for choosing this book as your guide, and we wish you every success in your graphics programming endeavors.

Printed in Great Britain
by Amazon

37878260R00136